BObBy DaZzler's
MAKE YOUR OWN
Misfits

BObBy DaZzler's

MAKE YOUR OWN

Misfits

35 unique and quirky sewn creatures

FUMIE KAMIJO and ROSIE SHORT

CICO BOOKS
LONDON NEW YORK

Published in 2010 by CICO Books
An imprint of Ryland Peters & Small Ltd
20–21 Jockey's Fields   519 Broadway, 5th Floor
London WC1R 4BW   New York, NY 10012

www.cicobooks.com

10 9 8 7 6 5 4 3 2 1

A CIP catalog record for this book is available from the
Library of Congress and the British Library.

ISBN-13: 978 1 907030 27 7

Printed in China

Editors: Jane Bolsover and Pete Jorgensen
Design concept: Luis Peral-Aranda
Design: Luis Peral-Aranda and Barbara Zuñiga
Photographer: Geoff Dann
Illustration: Rosie Short and Fumie Kamijo

CONTENTS

INTRODUCTION

The world of Bobby Dazzler, that's the name we give our rag-tag collection of misfits, is a strange, beguiling, and intriguing one packed full of entertainers, explorers, animals, and eccentrics. Many have had charmed lives, some perhaps have not been quite as lucky, but all definitely have a story to tell!

Each misfit begins life at Bobby Dazzler HQ in London's East End, where they are hand-made by us, Fumie and Rosie. They also benefit from a bit of Far Eastern charm every now and again as Satoko, Fumie's mum back in Tokyo, likes to lend a hand in bringing new misfits into the world.

We get inspiration for the dolls from all over and we base them on anyone or anything that we come across going about our day to day lives. Over the years, we have made thousands of misfits and have collectors of all ages, shapes, and sizes from across the globe.

In the summer we go on a road trip out into the country in our vintage horse box, which magically turns into Bobby Dazzler's mobile home and curiosity shop. We take this to festivals where we hold workshops, teaching people how to create their own unique misfits that they can then keep for life.

After hosting a few of these workshops, the response was so great that people thought it was about time to share the misfit love and the result is this book. The 35 projects here aim to give everyone the opportunity to make their own collection of Bobby Dazzlers and demonstrate how easy they are to create. Once you have made a couple of misfits, why not start designing your own as well, basing them on anything you want—whether it's your dad, best friend, mail man, teacher, pet rock, or whatever. Once you have done so, why not visit our website at www.theworldofbobbydazzler.co.uk and send us a snap, we would love to see the ideas you come up with.

FUMIE AND ROSIE

Sourcing material

Every Bobby Dazzler we make starts off life as something else. It may have originally been a stripey tee shirt, a Christmas sweater knitted by someone's granny many moons ago, or an 80s day-glo jumpsuit that we thought should get another chance to shine. The thing that these materials have in common is that they have all been recycled. We like the idea of giving things that people throw away a new lease of life, and the used feel of pre-worn fabrics gives an extra bit of charm to a new-born misfit. Also, make sure you check old clothes for buttons and beads, these are essential items for a misfit makeover. Look out for logos on clothes as well. A great design on the center of a tee shirt can be used on the body of a misfit with a bit of planning and some careful cutting.

We've got a few choice places that we regularly go to source fabric for our creations, here's our top 3.

1. THRIFT STORES AND CHARITY SHOPS
These are a goldmine for unusual, weird, and wonderful fabrics. They are packed full of spots, stripes, checks, plaid, tweed, gingham, florals, suede, silks... the list goes on. And the best thing about thrift stores is that the prices are usually dirt cheap, so you can buy until your heart's content.

2. MARKETS
You can find all sorts of unexpected things at flea markets. We often stumble across the most beautiful buttons attached to jackets, coats, and jeans that we liberate and then use as eyes, noses, or mouths. Old-school pin badges are usually readily available and can be clipped on to a Bobby Dazzler's body—the perfect accessory!

3. YOUR OWN WARDROBE
You'll be surprised at what you find if you dig into the darkest depths of your closet. There'll be old shirts, shorts, and sweaters that you won't have worn for years—these are just gagging to be transformed into something new. If you're a horder who doesn't like throwing things away even better, because you won't have to part with any of your old clothes, you'll just turn them into something new instead.

DEN the penguin

Den is an old fashioned kind of chap. He loves to sing songs from the musicals and is happiest when he's ballroom dancing.

You will need...

BLACK SWEATER OR TEE SHIRT

SEWING MACHINE

NEEDLE AND MATCHING THREADS

WADDING

SCRAPS OF WHITE AND RED FELT

FABRIC GLUE

TWO WHITE BUTTONS

YELLOW SOCK

1

Using the templates on page 13, cut out two bodies from the sweater, two beaks from the sock, and one belly from white felt. With a ¼in (6mm) seam allowance, machine stitch the body pieces together, leaving a small opening for turning through.

Use an overhand stitch to sew up the opening in the body. Now he's ready for his makeover!

Turn the body right side out and fill with wadding by pushing small amounts through the opening until it is nicely shaped. Use a stick or pencil to help push the wadding into the arms and legs.

2

3

4 Machine stitch the beak pieces together, with a ¼in (6mm) seam allowance, leaving the straight edges open. Turn right side out and fill the beak with wadding.

5 Stitch the beak to Den's face using overhand stitch. Now he can talk and eat!

6 Using the photograph as a guide, stitch on the buttons for eyes and glue the belly in place. Leave to dry.

7 Using the template opposite, cut out a rectangle of red felt for Den's bow tie. Wrap thread around the center several times and stitch the bow tie in place under his beak. Doesn't he look smart?

DEN'S templates

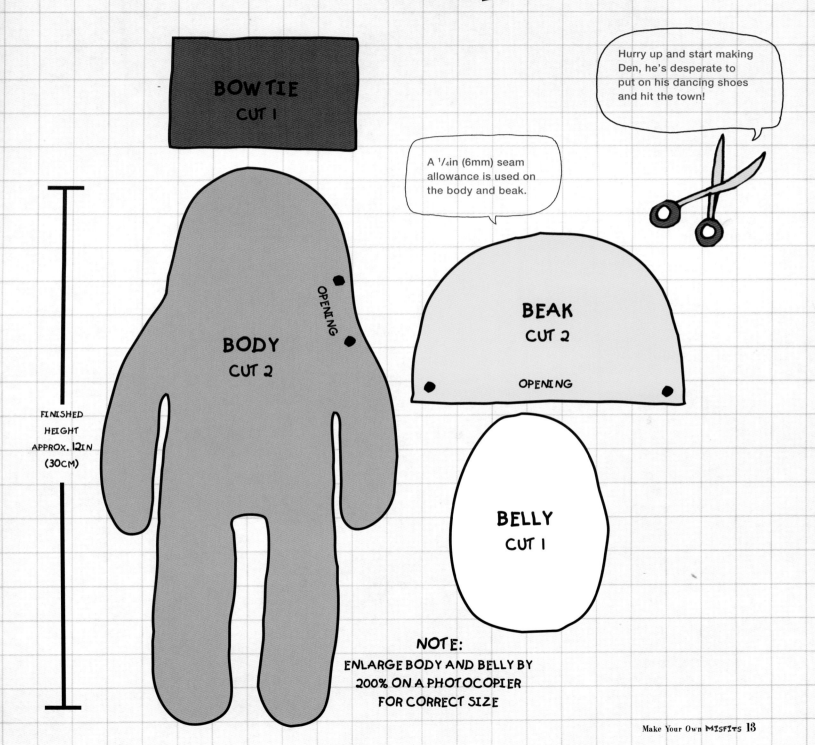

FREDDIE the mouse

Freddie spends his days in the garage polishing his car, dreaming of the open road. One day he'll take it for a drive but he needs to get his license first.

You will need...

STRIPY TEE SHIRT   SEWING MACHINE

MATCHING THREADS   WADDING

GRAY SWEATER   LARGE RED BUTTON AND BLACK BEADS

NEEDLE AND WHITE HEAVY-DUTY THREAD   SCRAP OF YELLOW FABRIC

1 Using the templates on page 17, cut out two bodies from the stripy tee shirt and two heads from the gray sweater. With a ¼in (6mm) seam allowance, machine stitch the matching pieces together, leaving a small opening in each piece.

2 Turn the body right side out and fill with wadding by pushing small amounts through the opening until it is nicely shaped. Use a stick or pencil to help push the wadding into the arms and legs. Do the same with the head.

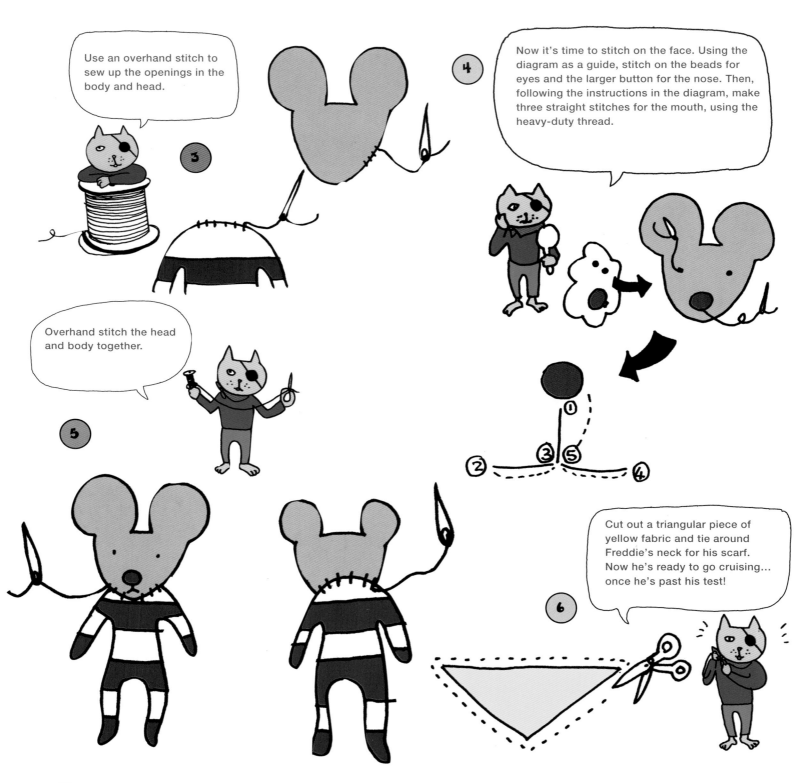

Use an overhand stitch to sew up the openings in the body and head.

3

Now it's time to stitch on the face. Using the diagram as a guide, stitch on the beads for eyes and the larger button for the nose. Then, following the instructions in the diagram, make three straight stitches for the mouth, using the heavy-duty thread.

4

Overhand stitch the head and body together.

5

Cut out a triangular piece of yellow fabric and tie around Freddie's neck for his scarf. Now he's ready to go cruising... once he's past his test!

6

A ¼in (6mm) seam allowance is used on both templates.

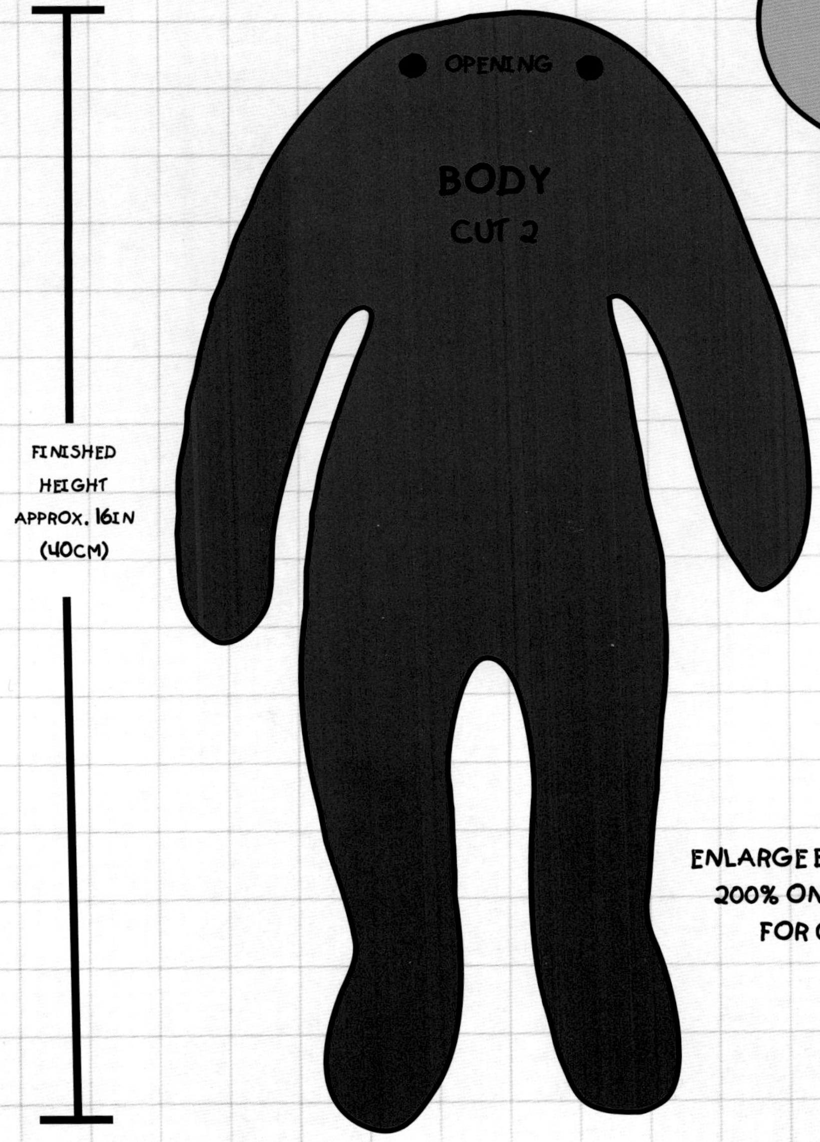

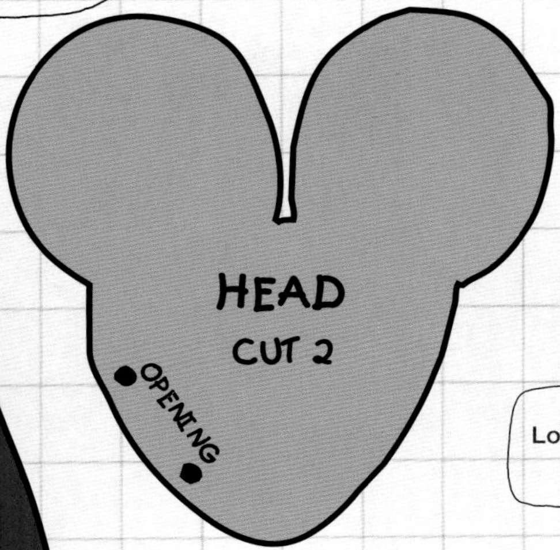

BODY
CUT 2

OPENING

HEAD
CUT 2

OPENING

Look at me go!

FINISHED HEIGHT APPROX. 16IN (40CM)

NOTE:
ENLARGE BODY AND HEAD BY 200% ON A PHOTOCOPIER FOR CORRECT SIZE

BETTY the butterfly

Betty flutters around all day
simply daydreaming.

You will need...

STRIPY SOCK

SEWING MACHINE

NEEDLE AND BLACK
THREAD

WADDING

MATCHING THREAD

SMALL BEADS

PURPLE AND YELLOW FELT

Using the template on page 20, cut out two bodies from the stripy sock. Taking a ¼in (6mm) seam allowance, machine stitch the pieces together, leaving a small opening.

1

Turn the body right side out and fill it with wadding by pushing small amounts through the opening until it is nicely shaped. Use an overhand stitch to sew up the opening.

2

3

Now it's time to stitch on the face. Using the photograph as a guide, stitch two black beads on for eyes and make a small black stitch for the mouth. Cut out a tiny rectangle from the scrap of purple felt, wrap thread around the center to form the bow tie, and stitch in place below the mouth.

Using the template on page 20, cut out the wings from yellow felt and attach to the back of Betty's body using a running stitch—watch as she flutters off into the sky!

4

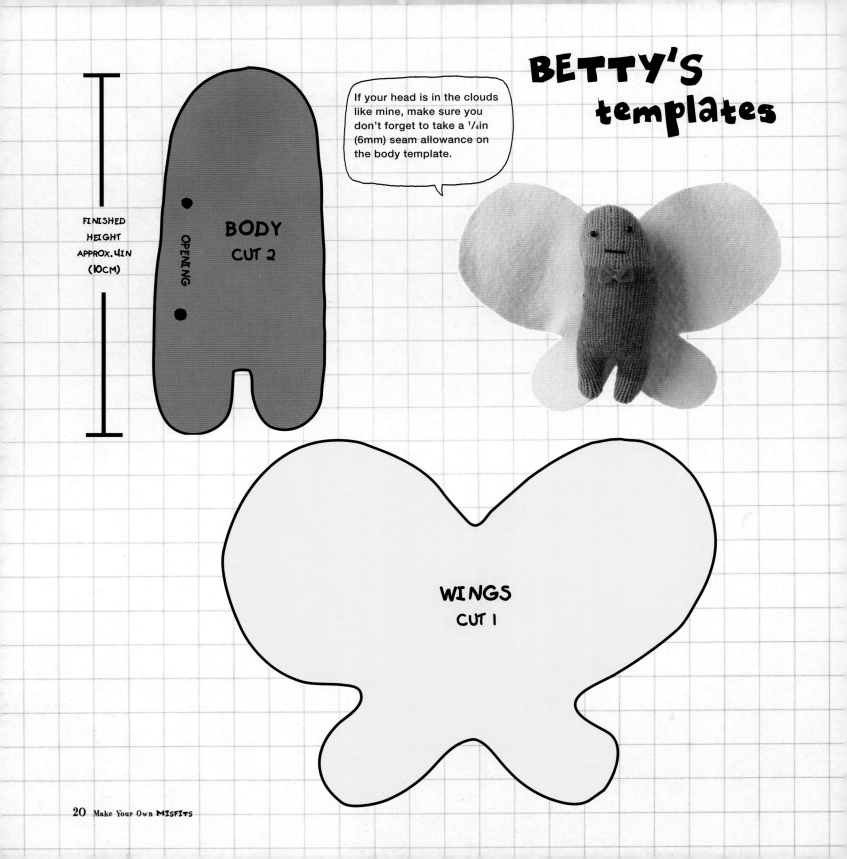

BETTY'S templates

FINISHED
HEIGHT
APPROX. 4IN
(10CM)

OPENING

BODY
CUT 2

If your head is in the clouds like mine, make sure you don't forget to take a 1/4in (6mm) seam allowance on the body template.

WINGS
CUT 1

FRANÇOIS the incredible frog

François is always looking for adventure. He loves to Irish dance and when he's in full swing his legs move so fast they simply become a blur!

You will need...

GREEN TEE SHIRT

SEWING MACHINE

NEEDLE AND BLACK THREAD

WADDING

MATCHING THREAD

TWO WHITE BUTTONS

SCRAP OF GLITTERY FABRIC

FABRIC PEN

WHITE HEAVY-DUTY THREAD

1 Using the template on page 23, cut out two bodies. Taking a ¼in (6mm) seam allowance, machine stitch the pieces together, leaving a small opening for turning through.

2 Turn the body right side out and fill with wadding by pushing small amounts through the opening until it is nicely shaped. Use a stick or a pen to help push the wadding into the arms and legs. Use overhand stitch to sew up the opening.

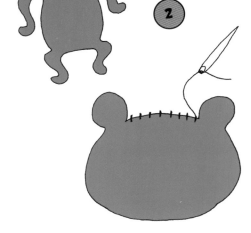

3 Now it's time to stitch on the face. Using the photograph as a guide, stitch the buttons on for eyes using the black thread and make a large stitch below for the mouth using the heavy-duty white thread.

4 Using the fabric pen draw on François' nostrils. Cut out a small triangle of glittery fabric for a scarf and tie around his neck. Now he's ready for some adventures!

FRANÇOIS' templates

Je suis le plus vite grenouille dansant du monde.

A ¼in (6mm) seam allowance is included when you cut me out.

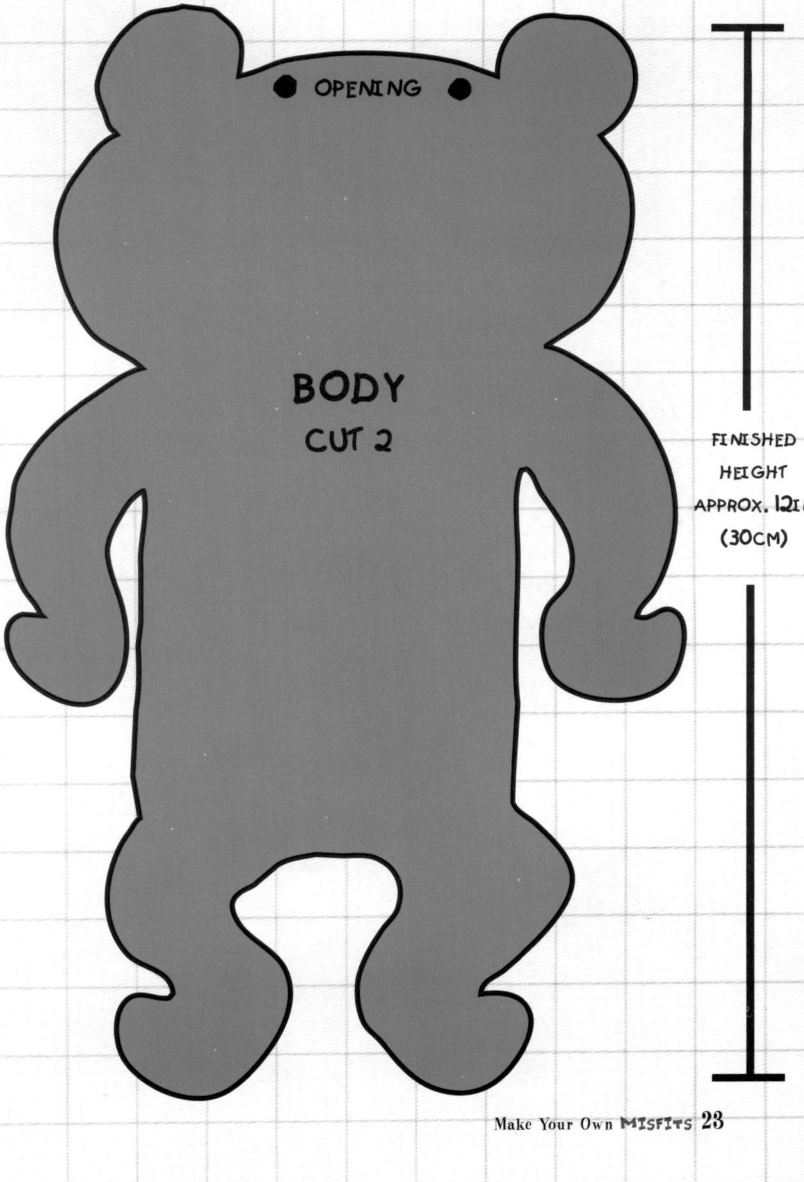

NOTE:
ENLARGE BODY BY 200% ON A PHOTOCOPIER FOR CORRECT SIZE

OPENING

BODY
CUT 2

FINISHED HEIGHT APPROX. 12IN (30CM)

DUMPLING
the guinea pig

Dumpling is a very shy creature, so you'll have to listen very carefully as his voice is so quiet. Make sure you do though because he's got some pretty interesting things to say.

1 Using the template on page 25, cut out two bodies from the fur fabric. Taking a ¼in (6mm) seam allowance, machine stitch the pieces together, leaving a small opening for turning through.

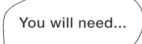

You will need...

FUR FABRIC SEWING MACHINE

MATCHING THREAD WADDING

PEARLY BUTTON AND BLACK BEADS NEEDLE AND BLACK HEAVY-DUTY THREAD

Turn the body right side out and fill with wadding by pushing small amounts through the opening until it is nicely shaped. Use a stick or pencil to help push the wadding into the arms and legs. Use overhand stitch to sew up the opening.

2

Now it's time to stitch on the face. Using the photograph as a guide, stitch on the beads for the eyes and the larger button below for his nose. Then, following the diagram and using heavy-duty thread, make three straight stitches for the mouth. Now he's all ready to go, but be gentle with him, remember he's not very confident.

3

DUMPLING's templates

A ¼in (6mm) seam allowance is included.

OPENING

BODY
CUT 2

FINISHED HEIGHT 9IN (22.5CM)

NOTE:
ENLARGE BODY BY 200% ON A PHOTOCOPIER FOR CORRECT SIZE

ALPHONSO the moose

Alphonso might seem a little strange at times, but he's just playing with his imaginary friends. He loves foraging in forests and uses his keen sense of smell to snaffle out treats.

You will need...

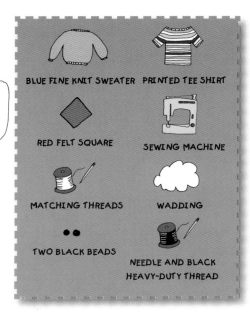

BLUE FINE KNIT SWEATER   PRINTED TEE SHIRT

RED FELT SQUARE   SEWING MACHINE

MATCHING THREADS   WADDING

TWO BLACK BEADS   NEEDLE AND BLACK HEAVY-DUTY THREAD

Using the templates on page 29, cut out two bodies from the tee shirt, two heads from the sweater, and two noses from the felt. With a ¼in (6mm) seam allowance, machine stitch the matching pieces together, leaving a small opening in each piece.

1

Turn the body right side out and fill with wadding by pushing small amounts through the opening until it is nicely shaped. Use a stick or pencil to help push the wadding into the arms and legs. Do the same with the head and nose.

2

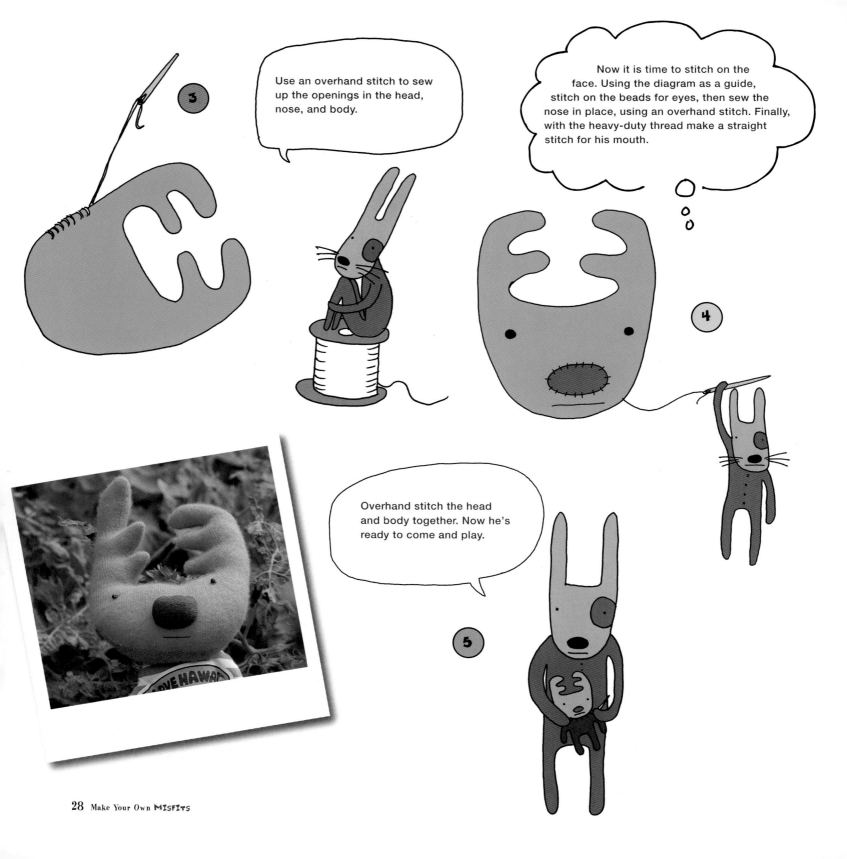

Use an overhand stitch to sew up the openings in the head, nose, and body.

3

Now it is time to stitch on the face. Using the diagram as a guide, stitch on the beads for eyes, then sew the nose in place, using an overhand stitch. Finally, with the heavy-duty thread make a straight stitch for his mouth.

4

Overhand stitch the head and body together. Now he's ready to come and play.

5

ALPHONSO's templates

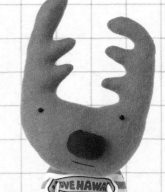

What do you mean, you can't see my imaginery friends? There's one sat right next to me!

NOTE:
ENLARGE BODY AND HEAD BY
200% ON A PHOTOCOPIER
FOR CORRECT SIZE

● OPENING ●
NOSE
CUT 2

A ¼in (6mm) seam allowance is included on all templates.

● OPENING ●
BODY
CUT 2

FINISHED HEIGHT APPROX. 15IN (37.5CM)

● OPENING ●
HEAD
CUT 2

You will need...

PINK SOCK   SEWING MACHINE

MATCHING THREAD

WADDING

BLACK BEADS

NEEDLE AND BLACK
HEAVY-DUTY THREAD

BERNIE, GEORGE, and DENZIL the worms

These lads are always busy, worming their way around. They are very popular with organic gardeners, as their wiggling ways do great things to soil!

Using the templates on page 31, cut out two of each body shape from the sock. With a ¼in (6mm) seam allowance, machine stitch the matching pieces together, leaving a small opening in each piece.

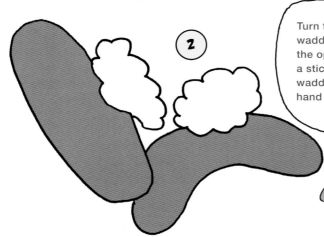

(2) Turn the bodies right side out and fill with wadding by pushing small amounts through the openings until they are nicely filled. Use a stick or pencil to help you push the wadding down into the bodies. Use overhand stitch to sew up the openings.

Now it's time to stitch on their faces. Using the photograph as a guide, sew on beads for the eyes and using the heavy-duty thread make, a single straight stitch for each mouth. Now watch them wiggle away into the sunset!

(3)

BERNIE, GEORGE, and DENZIL's templates

NOTE:
ENLARGE BODIES BY 200% ON A PHOTOCOPIER FOR CORRECT SIZE

A ¼in (6mm) seam allowance is included on all templates.

OPENING

OPENING

OPENING

FINISHED HEIGHT APPROX. 4IN (10CM)

BODIES
CUT 2 FOR EACH WORM

WISE the badger

Wise is whom all the Bobby Dazzlers go to if they find they have a problem. He can answer any question you ask him and is a dab hand at DIY, too.

You will need...

GRAY TEE SHIRT

WHITE FLEECE SWEATER

SEWING MACHINE

MATCHING THREADS

WADDING

BLACK FABRIC PAINT AND BRUSH

TWO SHIRT BUTTONS AND LARGE BLACK BEAD

NEEDLE AND THREAD

Using the templates on page 35, cut out two bodies from the tee shirt and two heads from the fleece. With a ¼in (6mm) seam allowance, machine stitch the matching pieces together, leaving a small opening in each piece.

1

Turn the body right side out and fill with wadding by pushing small amounts through the opening until it is nicely shaped. Use a stick or pencil to help push the wadding into the arms and legs. Do the same with his head.

2

Use an overhand stitch to sew up the openings in the head and body.

3

Using the photograph and diagram as a guide, paint the stripes on to the face with black fabric paint and leave to dry.

When dry, you can stitch on the face. Once again, using the diagram as a guide, stitch on the buttons for eyes and sew the large bead on the end of the face for his nose.

Overhand stitch the head and body together. Now remember, if you ever have a problem, Wise badger is sure to be able to help out.

wISE's templates

A ¼in (6mm) seam allowance is included on both templates.

You can't fool me, Dennis!

HEAD
CUT 2

OPENING

BODY
CUT 2

OPENING

NOTE:
ENLARGE BOTH TEMPLATES BY 200% ON A PHOTOCOPIER FOR CORRECT SIZE

FINISHED HEIGHT APPROX. 14IN (35CM)

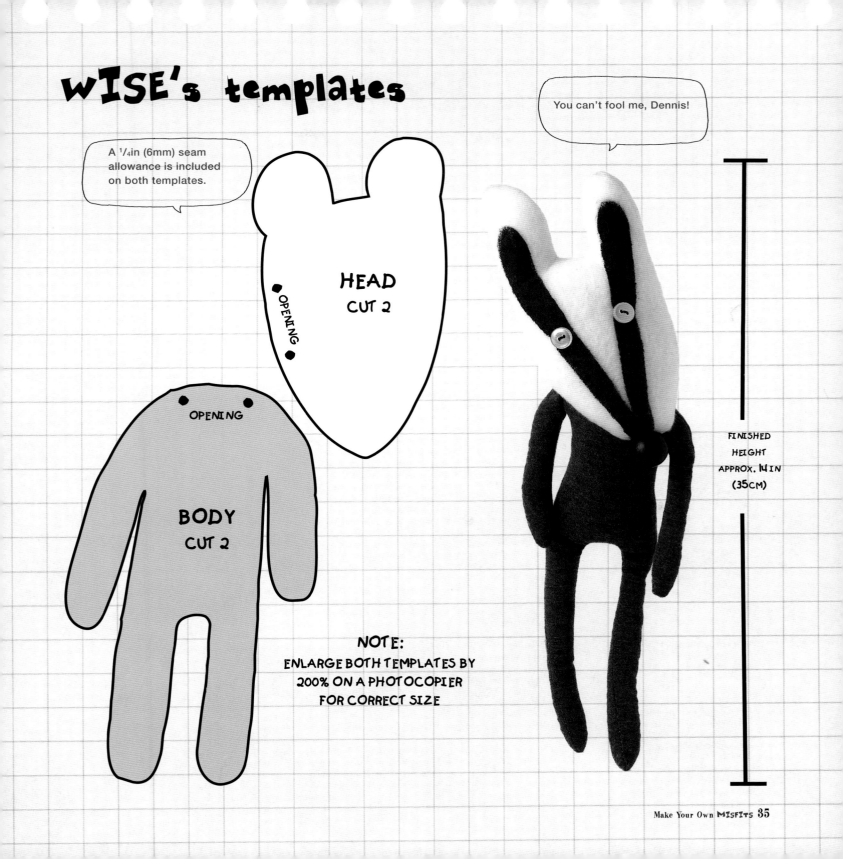

MONTY the giraffe

Oh Monty! He's always sticking his nose into other people's business. Snooping around corners and gossiping over the garden fence, he really is such a troublemaker.

You will need...

GREEN FLEECE SWEATER

CREAM TEE SHIRT

SEWING MACHINE

MATCHING THREADS

WADDING

NEEDLE AND BLACK HEAVY-DUTY THREAD

TWO BEADS OR SMALL BUTTONS

PINK FELT

Using the templates on page 39, cut out two bodies from the fleece and two heads from the tee shirt. With a ¼in (6mm) seam allowance, machine stitch the matching pieces together, leaving a small opening in each piece.

1

Turn the body right side out and fill with wadding by pushing small amounts through the opening until it is nicely shaped. Use a stick or pencil to help push the wadding into the arms and legs. Do the same with the head.

2

Use an overhand stitch to sew up the opening in the body. Fold under the raw edges on the neck end of the head and sew the head to the top of the body using overhand stitch.

Now it's time to stitch on the face. Using the diagram as a guide, stitch on the beads or buttons for eyes, and using the heavy-duty thread make a couple of large straight stitches for the mouth.

3

4

5

Finally, he needs a nice big bow tie. Using the template opposite, cut out a rectangle from felt. Wrap the heavy-duty thread tightly around the center to create a bow tie shape; stitch to base of neck. Now doesn't he look a real bobby dazzler, but watch out, trouble follows him wherever he goes!

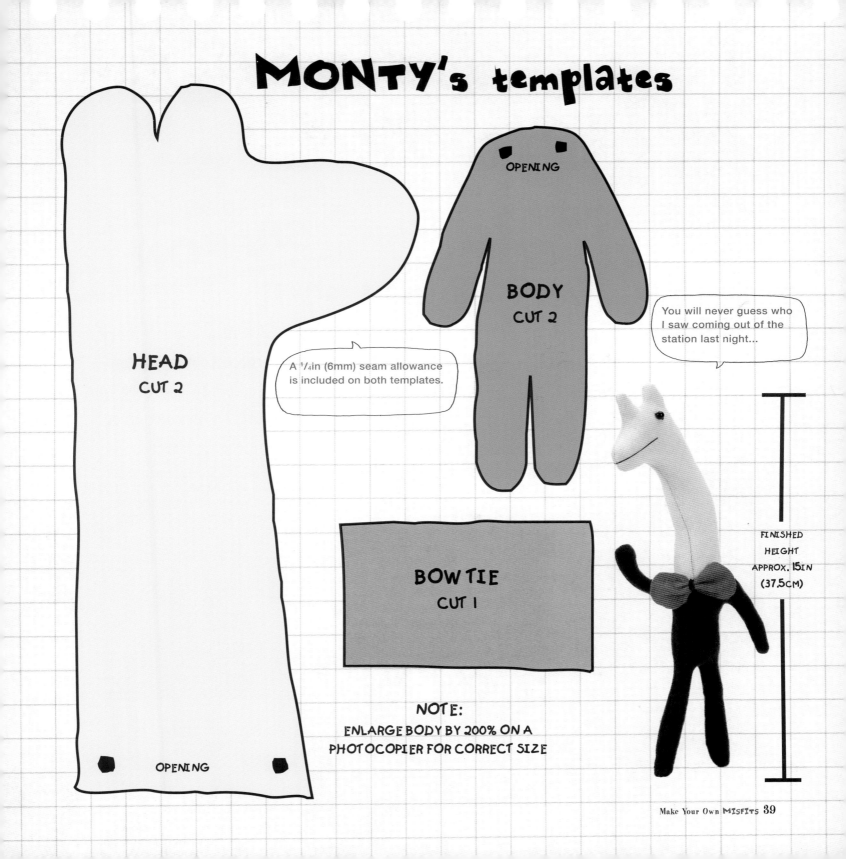

MONTY's templates

HEAD
CUT 2

OPENING

BODY
CUT 2

OPENING

A ¼in (6mm) seam allowance is included on both templates.

You will never guess who I saw coming out of the station last night...

BOW TIE
CUT 1

FINISHED HEIGHT APPROX. 15IN (37.5CM)

OPENING

NOTE:
ENLARGE BODY BY 200% ON A PHOTOCOPIER FOR CORRECT SIZE

SHARON

the sheep

Sharon is tired of following the herd, she now wants to be an independent woman. She has moved to the city and loves to go shopping in Woolworths.

Using the templates on page 42, cut out two bodies from the fleece and two heads and two tails from the tee shirt. With a ¼in (6mm) seam allowance, machine stitch the matching pieces together, leaving a small opening in each piece.

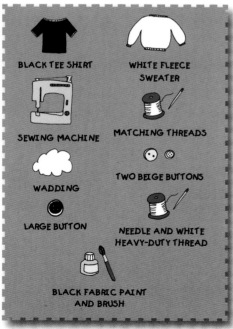

BLACK TEE SHIRT

WHITE FLEECE SWEATER

SEWING MACHINE

MATCHING THREADS

WADDING

TWO BEIGE BUTTONS

LARGE BUTTON

NEEDLE AND WHITE HEAVY-DUTY THREAD

BLACK FABRIC PAINT AND BRUSH

You will need...

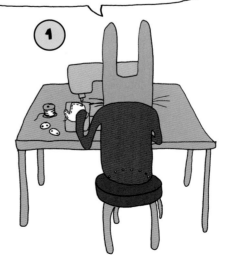

1

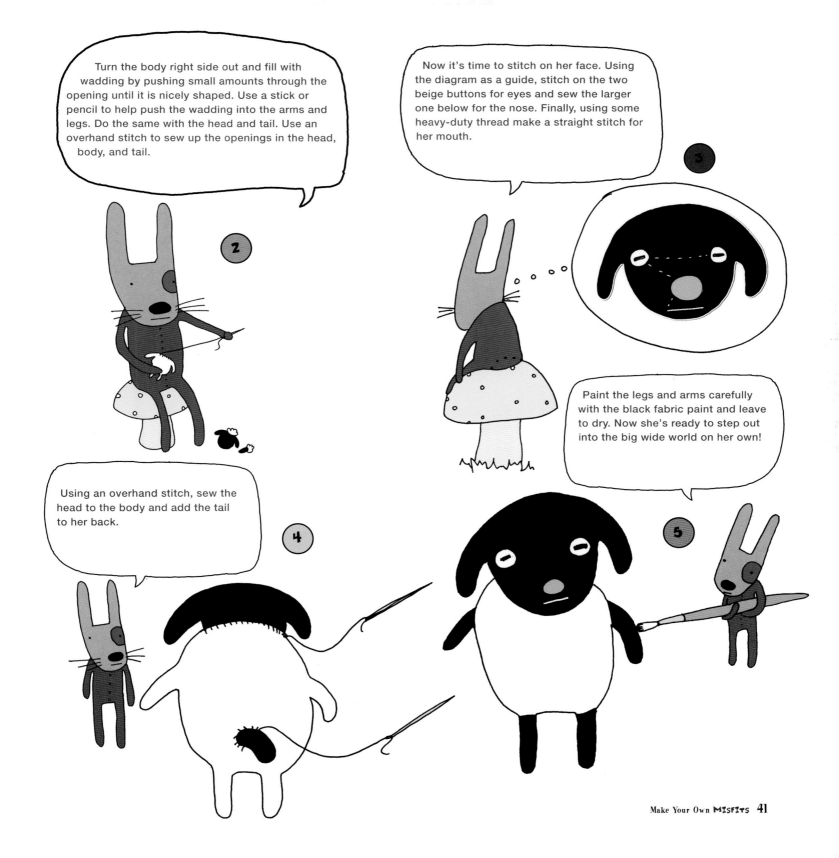

SHARON's templates

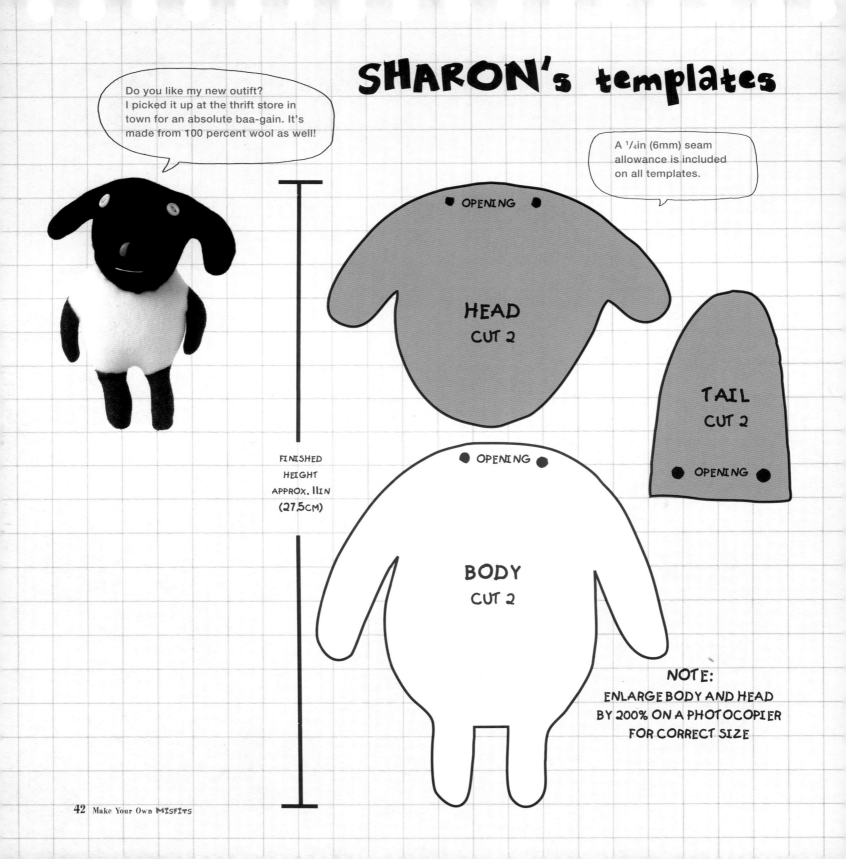

Do you like my new outift? I picked it up at the thrift store in town for an absolute baa-gain. It's made from 100 percent wool as well!

A ¼in (6mm) seam allowance is included on all templates.

OPENING

HEAD
CUT 2

TAIL
CUT 2

OPENING

FINISHED
HEIGHT
APPROX. 11IN
(27.5CM)

OPENING

BODY
CUT 2

NOTE:
ENLARGE BODY AND HEAD
BY 200% ON A PHOTOCOPIER
FOR CORRECT SIZE

You will need...

 WHITE FLEECE SWEATER

 SEWING MACHINE

 MATCHING THREAD

 WADDING

 TWO BLACK BUTTONS

NEEDLE AND BLACK HEAVY-DUTY THREAD

 LARGE GREEN BUTTON

BLACK FABRIC PAINT AND FINE BRUSH

Dorothy the Dalmatian

Dorothy is happiest when she's out on a walk or sitting on your lap. Her life ambition is to walk the length of the Great Wall of China with her friends.

Using the templates on page 45, cut out two bodies and two heads from the fleece. With a ¼in (6mm) seam allowance, machine stitch the matching pieces together, leaving a small opening in each piece.

1

Turn the body right side out and fill with wadding by pushing small amounts through the opening until it is nicely shaped. Use a stick or pencil to help push the wadding into the arms and legs. Do the same with the head.

2

Use an overhand stitch to sew up the openings in the head and body.

3

Now it's time to stitch on her face. Using the diagram as a guide, stitch the black buttons on for eyes and the green button on for the nose. Finally, with the heavy-duty thread make a straight stitch underneath for her mouth.

4

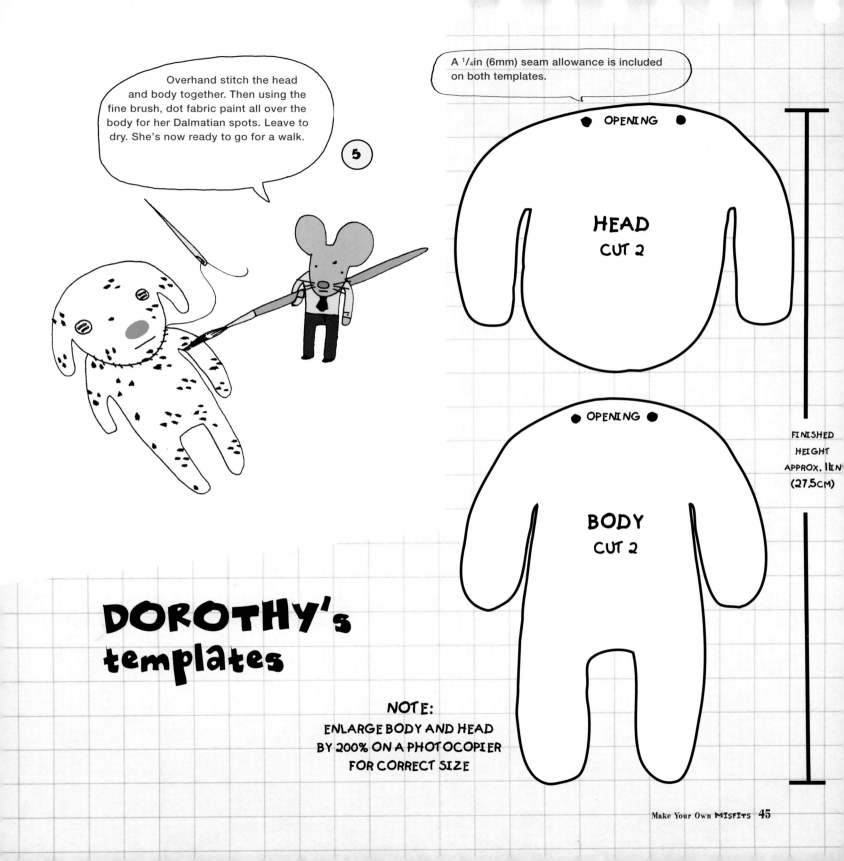

Overhand stitch the head and body together. Then using the fine brush, dot fabric paint all over the body for her Dalmatian spots. Leave to dry. She's now ready to go for a walk.

5

A ¼in (6mm) seam allowance is included on both templates.

● OPENING ●

HEAD
CUT 2

● OPENING ●

BODY
CUT 2

FINISHED HEIGHT APPROX. 11IN (27.5CM)

DOROTHY's templates

NOTE:
ENLARGE BODY AND HEAD
BY 200% ON A PHOTOCOPIER
FOR CORRECT SIZE

ELSIE the elephant

Elsie simply loves to ballet dance, but unfortunately she's so clumsy and has no rhythm, which means she's not the most elegant performer on stage.

You will need...

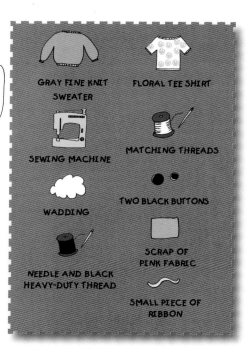

GRAY FINE KNIT SWEATER

FLORAL TEE SHIRT

SEWING MACHINE

MATCHING THREADS

WADDING

TWO BLACK BUTTONS

NEEDLE AND BLACK HEAVY-DUTY THREAD

SCRAP OF PINK FABRIC

SMALL PIECE OF RIBBON

Using the templates on page 49, cut out two heads, two trunks, and two pairs of ears from the gray sweater plus two bodies from the tee shirt. Taking a ¼in (6mm) seam allowance, machine stitch the matching pieces together, leaving a small opening in each piece.

Turn the body right side out and fill with wadding by pushing small amounts through the opening until it is nicely shaped. Use a stick or a pen to help push the wadding into the arms and legs. Do the same with Elsie's head, trunk, and ears.

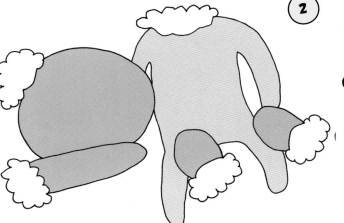

Use an overhand stitch to sew up the openings in the head, trunk, ears, and body.

3

Now it's time to stitch on her face. Use overhand stitch to attach the ears and trunk. Using the diagram as a guide, stitch the black buttons on for eyes. Finally, with the heavy-duty thread make a straight stitch underneath for her mouth.

4

Using the template opposite, cut two rectangles from pink fabric. Taking a ¼in (6mm) seam allowance, machine stitch the pieces together, leaving a small opening. Turn bow right side out and tightly wrap the ribbon around the center; sew it to the top of Elsie's head—now she's ready to go, but don't laugh at her dancing, as it will all end in tears!

5

Overhand stitch the head and body together.

6

ELSIE's templates

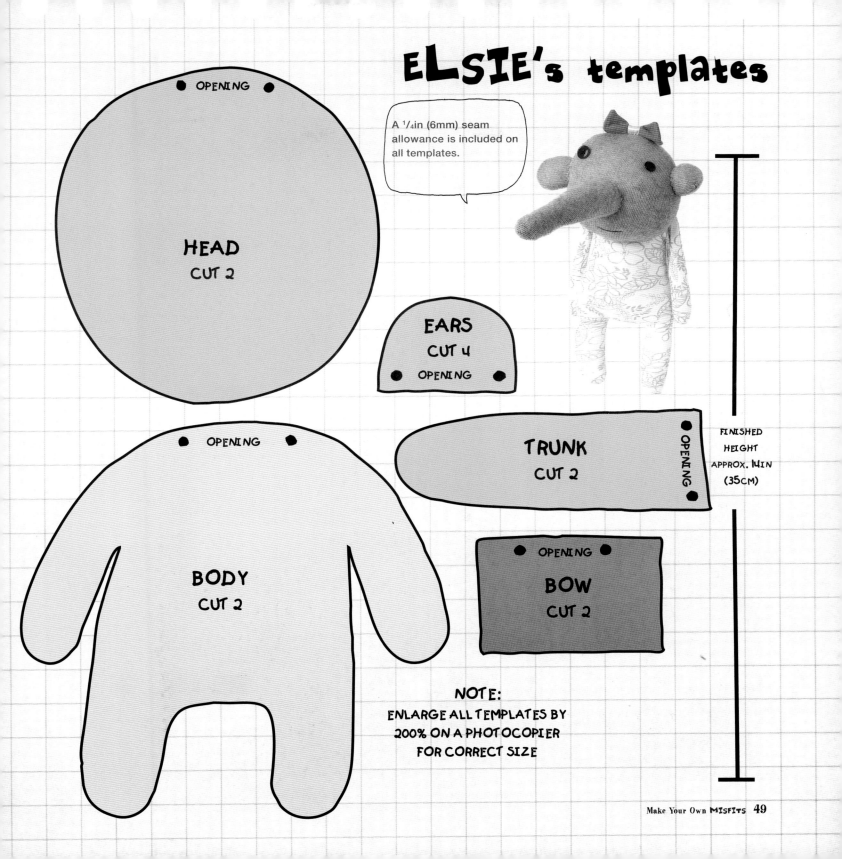

● OPENING ●

HEAD
CUT 2

A ¹/₄in (6mm) seam allowance is included on all templates.

EARS
CUT 4
● OPENING ●

● OPENING ●

BODY
CUT 2

TRUNK
CUT 2
OPENING

FINISHED HEIGHT APPROX. 14IN (35CM)

● OPENING ●

BOW
CUT 2

NOTE:
ENLARGE ALL TEMPLATES BY 200% ON A PHOTOCOPIER FOR CORRECT SIZE

ALICE the cuddly piglet

Alice is a bit mucky because she loves rolling around in the mud and dirt but, every Sunday she has a rosy bubble bath, and when she comes out she's the cuddliest thing you ever did see.

You will need...

PINK FINE KNIT SWEATER

SEWING MACHINE

MATCHING THREAD

WADDING

NEEDLE AND BLACK HEAVY-DUTY THREAD

BLACK BEADS

FABRIC PEN

1 Using the templates on page 52, cut out two heads, two snouts, and two bodies from the pink sweater. Taking a ¼in (6mm) seam allowance, machine stitch the matching pieces together, leaving a small opening in each piece.

2 Turn the body right side out and fill with wadding by pushing small amounts through the opening until it is nicely shaped. Use a stick or a pen to help push the wadding into the arms and legs. Do the same with the snout and head.

3 Use an overhand stitch to sew up the openings in the head, body, and snout.

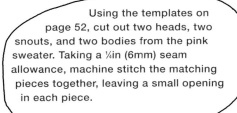

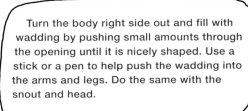

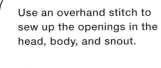

ALICE's templates

I always come up smelling of roses!

A ¼in (6mm) seam allowance is included on all templates.

OPENING

HEAD
CUT 2

FINISHED HEIGHT APPROX. 9IN (22.5CM)

OPENING

SNOUT
CUT 2

OPENING

BODY
CUT 2

NOTE:
ENLARGE ALL TEMPLATES BY 200% ON A PHOTOCOPIER FOR CORRECT SIZE

Now it's time to stitch on the face. Using the photograph as a guide, stitch on the two black beads for eyes and attach the snout below, using overhand stitch. Make a long black stitch below for the mouth using the heavy-duty thread and finally, draw the nostrils on to the snout using a fabric pen.

4

Overhand stitch the head and body together—keep an eye on her though, if she sees a muddy puddle she will be straight in it!

5

GRACIE the rabbit

You will need...

Gracie spends all her days skipping through the meadows collecting wild flowers, and greeting fairies as she goes.

RED FINE KNIT SWEATER

PINK TEE SHIRT

SEWING MACHINE

MATCHING THREAD

WADDING

BLACK BEADS

LARGE BUTTON

NEEDLE AND BLACK HEAVY-DUTY THREAD

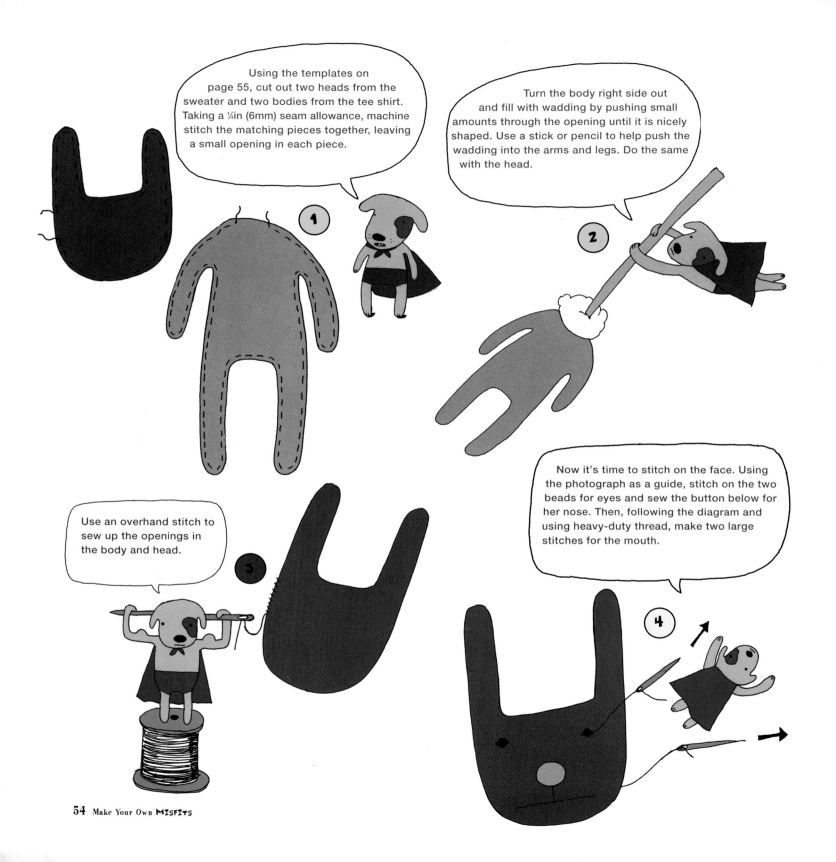

Using the templates on page 55, cut out two heads from the sweater and two bodies from the tee shirt. Taking a ¼in (6mm) seam allowance, machine stitch the matching pieces together, leaving a small opening in each piece.

1

Turn the body right side out and fill with wadding by pushing small amounts through the opening until it is nicely shaped. Use a stick or pencil to help push the wadding into the arms and legs. Do the same with the head.

2

Use an overhand stitch to sew up the openings in the body and head.

3

Now it's time to stitch on the face. Using the photograph as a guide, stitch on the two beads for eyes and sew the button below for her nose. Then, following the diagram and using heavy-duty thread, make two large stitches for the mouth.

4

Finally, overhand stitch the head and body together. Now, doesn't she look pretty!

5

GRACIE's templates

A ¼in (6mm) seam allowance is included on both templates.

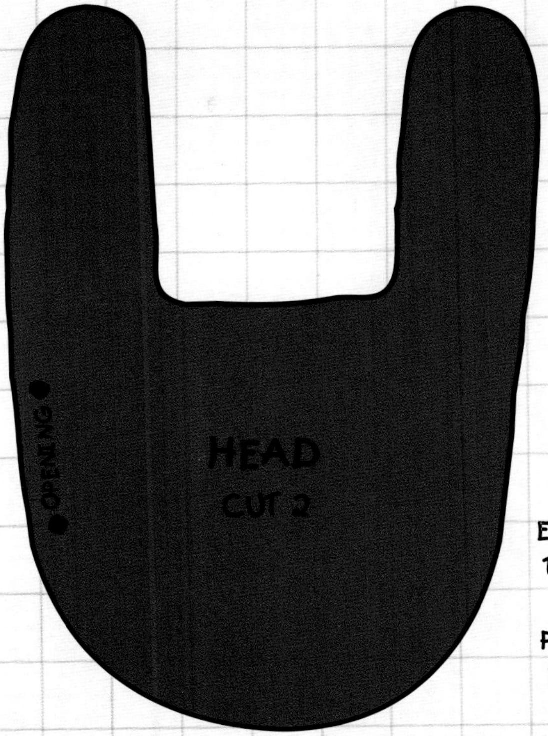

● OPENING ●

BODY
CUT 2

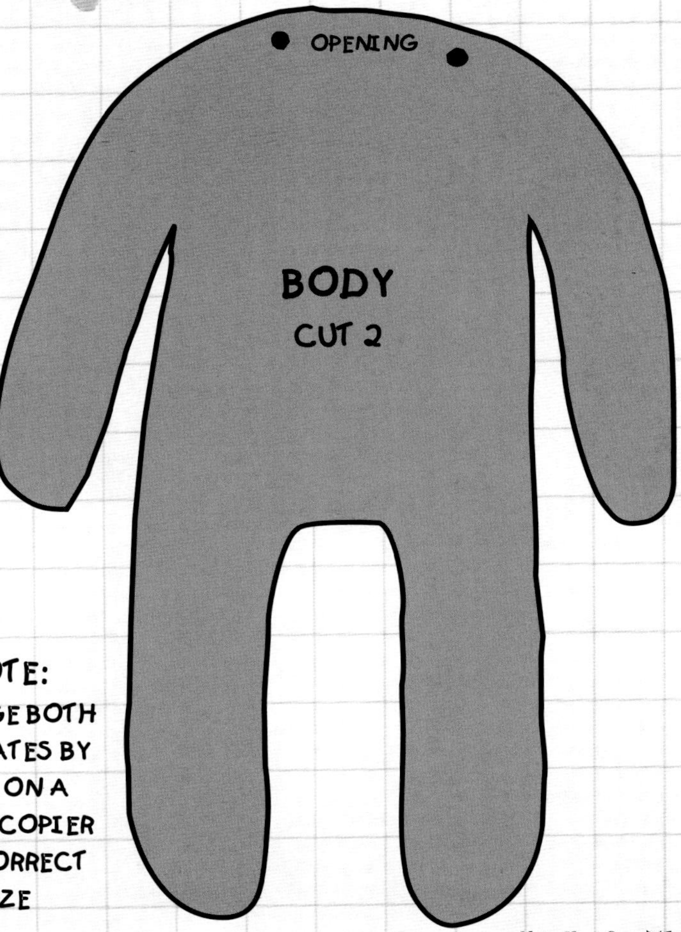

FINISHED HEIGHT APPROX 14IN (35CM)

● OPENING ●

HEAD
CUT 2

NOTE: ENLARGE BOTH TEMPLATES BY 200% ON A PHOTOCOPIER FOR CORRECT SIZE

LARRY the cat

Larry enjoys slinking around alleyways after dark just looking for kicks. He's a real night owl and knows all the best after hours jazz clubs around town.

1 Using the template opposite, cut out two bodies from the sweater. Taking a ¼in (6mm) seam allowance, machine stitch the pieces together, leaving a small opening for turning through.

You will need...

ORANGE FINE KNIT SWEATER

SEWING MACHINE

MATCHING THREAD

WADDING

TWO SHIRT BUTTONS

LARGE FLAT BUTTON

NEEDLE AND BLACK HEAVY-DUTY THREAD

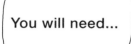
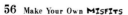

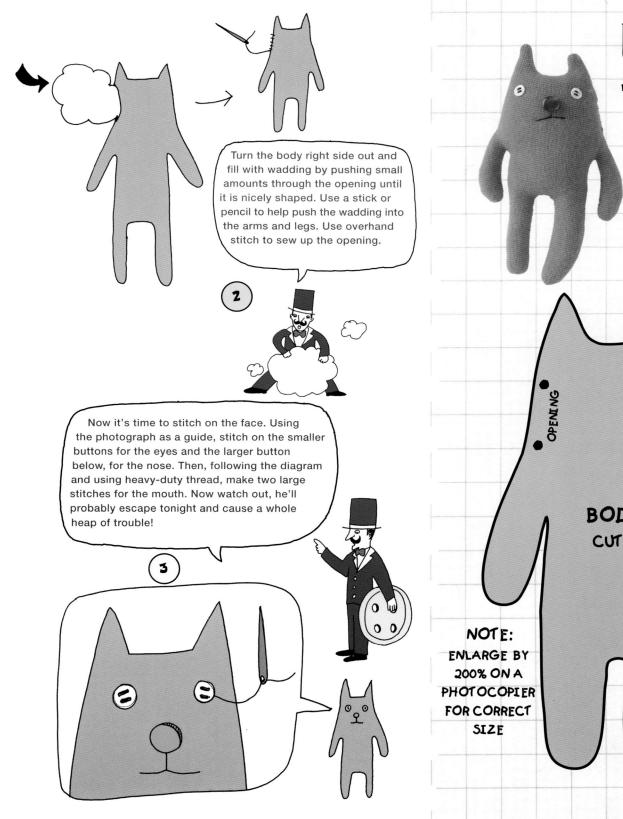

Turn the body right side out and fill with wadding by pushing small amounts through the opening until it is nicely shaped. Use a stick or pencil to help push the wadding into the arms and legs. Use overhand stitch to sew up the opening.

2

Now it's time to stitch on the face. Using the photograph as a guide, stitch on the smaller buttons for the eyes and the larger button below, for the nose. Then, following the diagram and using heavy-duty thread, make two large stitches for the mouth. Now watch out, he'll probably escape tonight and cause a whole heap of trouble!

3

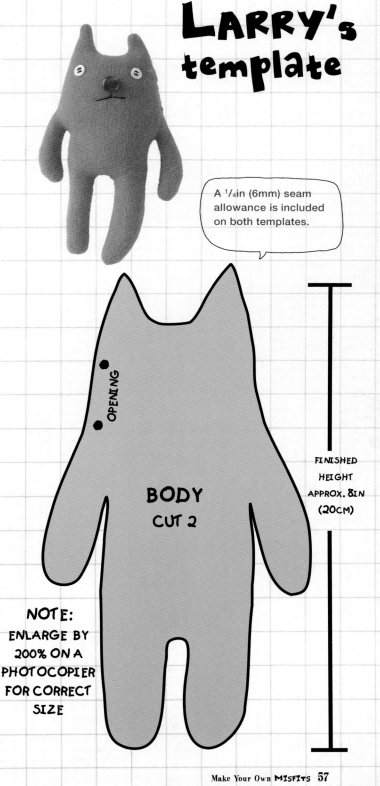

LARRY's template

A ¼in (6mm) seam allowance is included on both templates.

OPENING

BODY
CUT 2

FINISHED HEIGHT APPROX. 8IN (20CM)

NOTE:
ENLARGE BY 200% ON A PHOTOCOPIER FOR CORRECT SIZE

LUDIVIC
the koala

Ludivic is a math genius and university professor who likes to spend his days chewing eucalyptus and solving numerical challenges with his students.

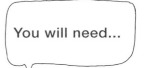

You will need...

RED TEE SHIRT

WHITE FINE KNIT SWEATER

BLACK SOCK

SEWING MACHINE

MATCHING THREAD

WHITE FUR FABRIC

WADDING

NEEDLE AND BLACK HEAVY-DUTY THREAD

TWO WHITE BUTTONS

TWO YELLOW BUTTONS

Using the templates on page 60, cut out two bodies from the tee shirt, two heads from the sweater, two noses from the sock, and four ears from the fur fabric. With a ¼in (6mm) seam allowance, machine stitch the matching pieces together, leaving a small opening in each piece.

Turn the body right side out and fill with wadding by pushing small amounts through the opening until it is nicely shaped. Use a stick or pencil to help push the wadding into the arms and legs. Do the same with the head, ears, and nose.

Use an overhand stitch to sew up the openings on the head, nose, and body.

Now it's time to stitch on the face. Using the diagram as a guide, stitch on the white buttons for eyes. Then, using overhand stitch, sew the nose in place and the open ends of the ears to each side of Ludivic's head. Finally, with the heavy-duty thread make a straight stitch for his mouth.

Overhand stitch the head and body together, and stitch the yellow buttons to the front of his body to make him look smart.

LUDIVIC's templates

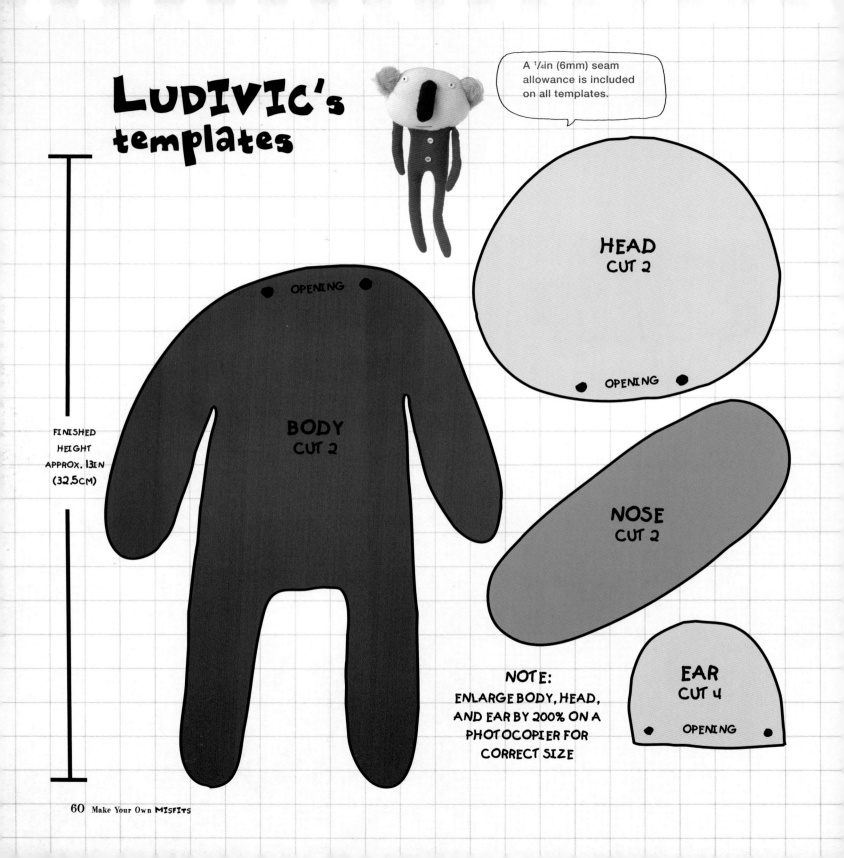

A ¼in (6mm) seam allowance is included on all templates.

HEAD
CUT 2

OPENING

OPENING

BODY
CUT 2

OPENING

FINISHED HEIGHT APPROX. 13IN (32.5CM)

NOSE
CUT 2

NOTE:
ENLARGE BODY, HEAD, AND EAR BY 200% ON A PHOTOCOPIER FOR CORRECT SIZE

EAR
CUT 4

OPENING

You will need...

GRAY VELOUR TOP   YELLOW TEE SHIRT

ORANGE SOCK   SEWING MACHINE

NEEDLE AND MATCHING THREADS   WADDING

TWO BLACK BEADS   RED FABRIC PEN

CHATTY the parrot

Chatty is learning English. He copies everything he hears, it's pretty annoying.

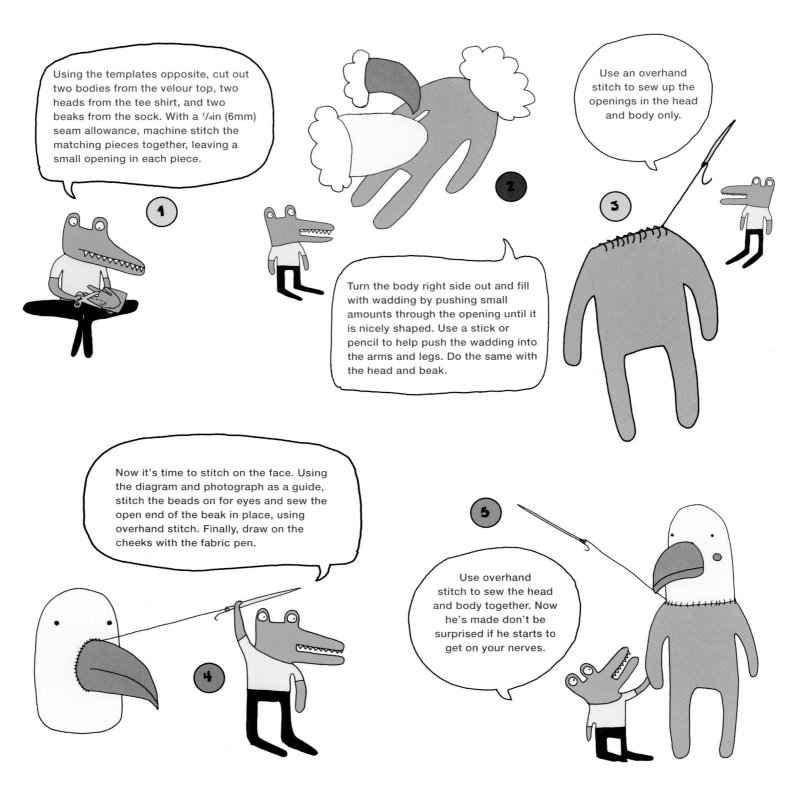

Using the templates opposite, cut out two bodies from the velour top, two heads from the tee shirt, and two beaks from the sock. With a ¼in (6mm) seam allowance, machine stitch the matching pieces together, leaving a small opening in each piece.

1

2

Turn the body right side out and fill with wadding by pushing small amounts through the opening until it is nicely shaped. Use a stick or pencil to help push the wadding into the arms and legs. Do the same with the head and beak.

Use an overhand stitch to sew up the openings in the head and body only.

3

Now it's time to stitch on the face. Using the diagram and photograph as a guide, stitch the beads on for eyes and sew the open end of the beak in place, using overhand stitch. Finally, draw on the cheeks with the fabric pen.

4

5

Use overhand stitch to sew the head and body together. Now he's made don't be surprised if he starts to get on your nerves.

CHATTY's templates

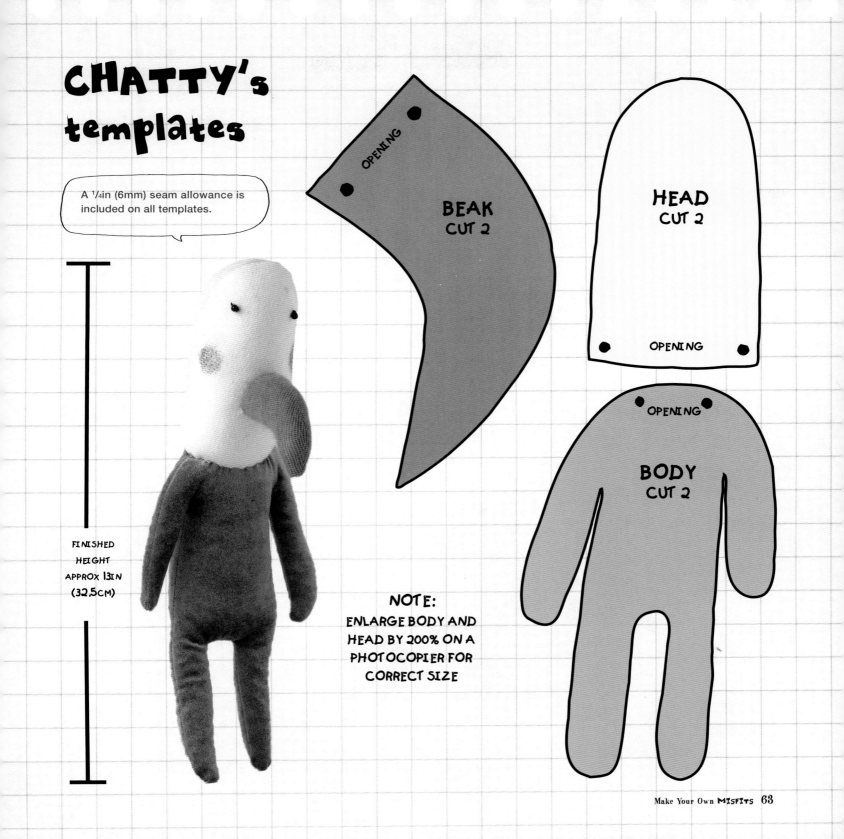

A ¼in (6mm) seam allowance is included on all templates.

BEAK
CUT 2

OPENING

HEAD
CUT 2

OPENING

OPENING

BODY
CUT 2

FINISHED HEIGHT APPROX 13IN (32.5CM)

NOTE:
ENLARGE BODY AND HEAD BY 200% ON A PHOTOCOPIER FOR CORRECT SIZE

DAVE
the slug

Dave has never done a
days work in his life, he
is such a lazy so and so.

You will need...

BLACK SOCK   SEWING MACHINE

MATCHING THREAD   WADDING

TWO SHIRT   NEEDLE AND WHITE
BUTTONS   HEAVY-DUTY THREAD

Using the template on page 65,
cut out two body shapes from the
sock. With a ¼in (6mm) seam
allowance, machine stitch the
pieces together, leaving a small
opening for turning through.

DAVE's templates

Turn the body right side out and fill with wadding by pushing small amounts through the opening until it is nicely shaped. Use a stick or pencil to help you push the wadding down into the body and his antennae. Use overhand stitch to sew up the opening.

Now it's time to stitch on Dave's face. Using the photograph as a guide, sew on the buttons for eyes and make a single straight stitch, using the heavy-duty thread, for his mouth. Now watch him as he just sits around all day doing absolutely nothing!

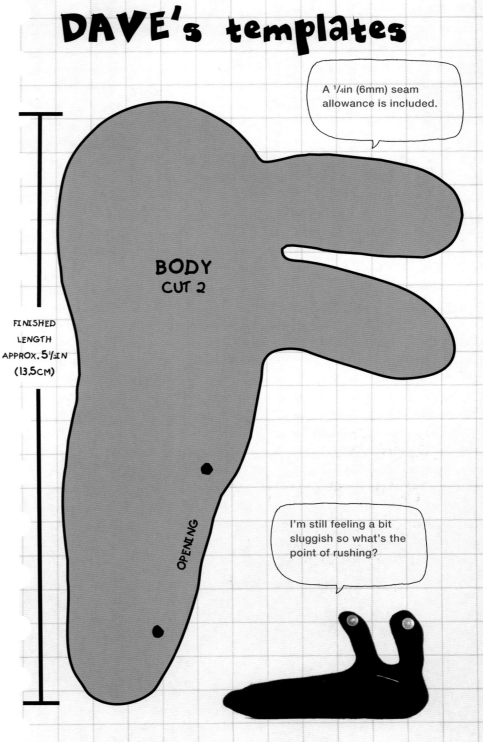

A ¼in (6mm) seam allowance is included.

BODY
CUT 2

FINISHED LENGTH APPROX. 5½IN (13.5CM)

OPENING

I'm still feeling a bit sluggish so what's the point of rushing?

MOO MOO
the owl

Moo Moo is a wise old bird, who loves thinking all sorts of thoughts.

You will need...

BEIGE SOCK

BROWN FINE KNIT SWEATER

SEWING MACHINE

MATCHING THREAD

WADDING

SCRAP OF WHITE FELT

FABRIC GLUE

NEEDLE AND THREAD

YELLOW BUTTONS

Using the templates on page 69, cut out two bodies and four wings from the sweater and two beaks from the sock. Taking a ¼in (6mm) seam allowance, machine stitch the matching pieces together, leaving small openings in each piece for turning through.

1

Turn the body right side out and fill with wadding by pushing small amounts through the opening until it is nicely shaped. Do the same with the beak. Turn the wings right side out, but leaved un-stuffed. Use overhand stitch to sew up each opening.

2

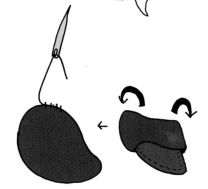

Stitch a button onto each felt circle for the eyes and using overhand stitch, attach the beak just below.

4

Now it's time to sort out his face. Using the templates opposite, cut out two circles from felt and using the photograph as a guide, glue the circles onto the face. Leave to dry.

3

Finally, sew a wing to each side of his body using overhand stitch. Now simply leave him to sit and think!

5

MOO MOO's templates

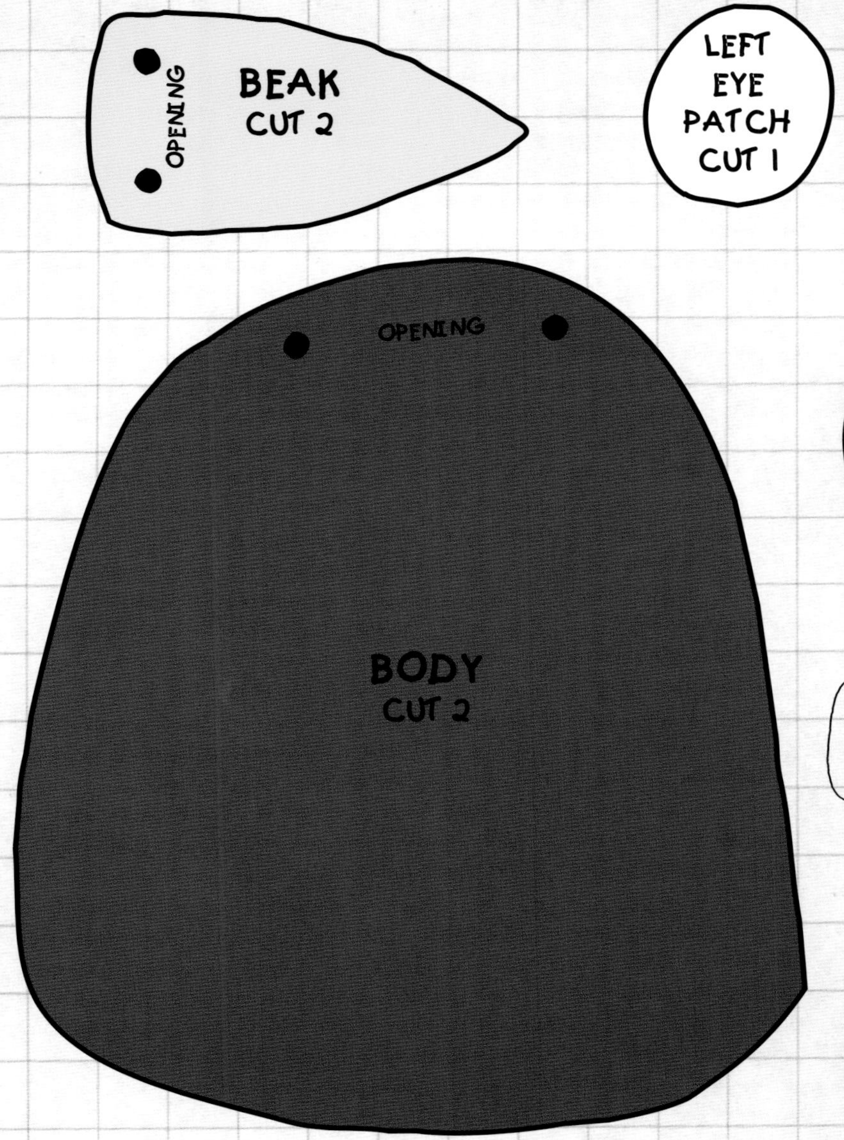

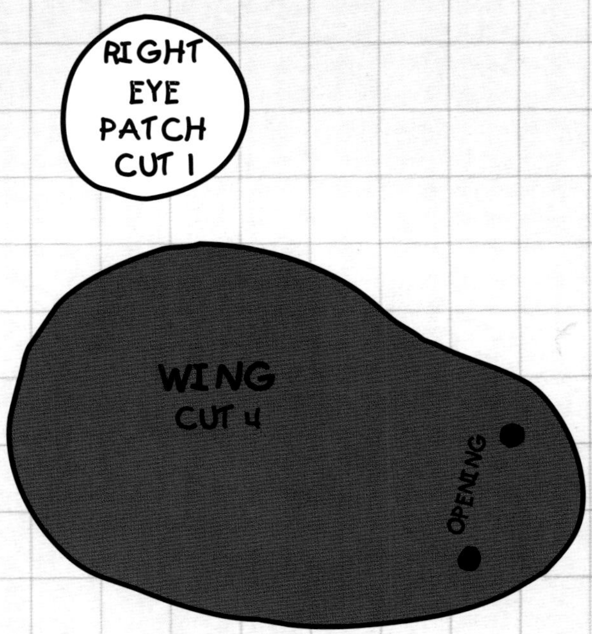

BEAK
CUT 2

OPENING

LEFT EYE PATCH CUT 1

RIGHT EYE PATCH CUT 1

BODY
CUT 2

OPENING

WING
CUT 4

OPENING

A ¼in (6mm) seam allowance is included on the body, wings, and beak.

FINISHED HEIGHT APPROX. 4IN (10CM)

HAMISH the bat

Poor old Hamish is out of sorts with his life and feeling a little bit lost. Hopefully when he gets a new home he'll start to feel much better once again.

You will need...

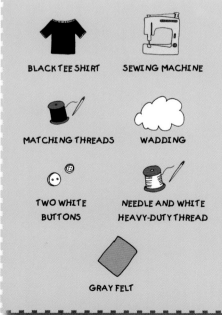

BLACK TEE SHIRT   SEWING MACHINE

MATCHING THREADS   WADDING

TWO WHITE BUTTONS   NEEDLE AND WHITE HEAVY-DUTY THREAD

GRAY FELT

Using the template on page 72, cut out two body shapes from the tee shirt. With a ¼in (6mm) seam allowance, machine stitch the pieces together, leaving a small opening for turning through.

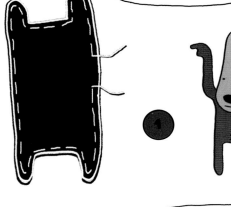

1

Turn the body right side out and fill with wadding by pushing small amounts through the opening until it is nicely shaped. Use overhand stitch to sew up the opening.

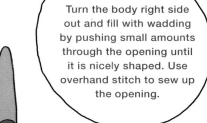

2

Now it's time to stitch on his face. Using the photograph as a guide, sew on buttons for the eyes and using heavy-duty thread make a single straight stitch for his mouth.

3

Using the template on page 72, cut out the wings from gray felt and attach them to the back of Hamish's body using a running stitch. He's sure now to be a friend for life!

4

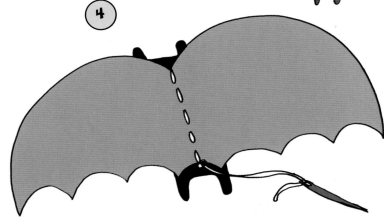

HAMISH's templates

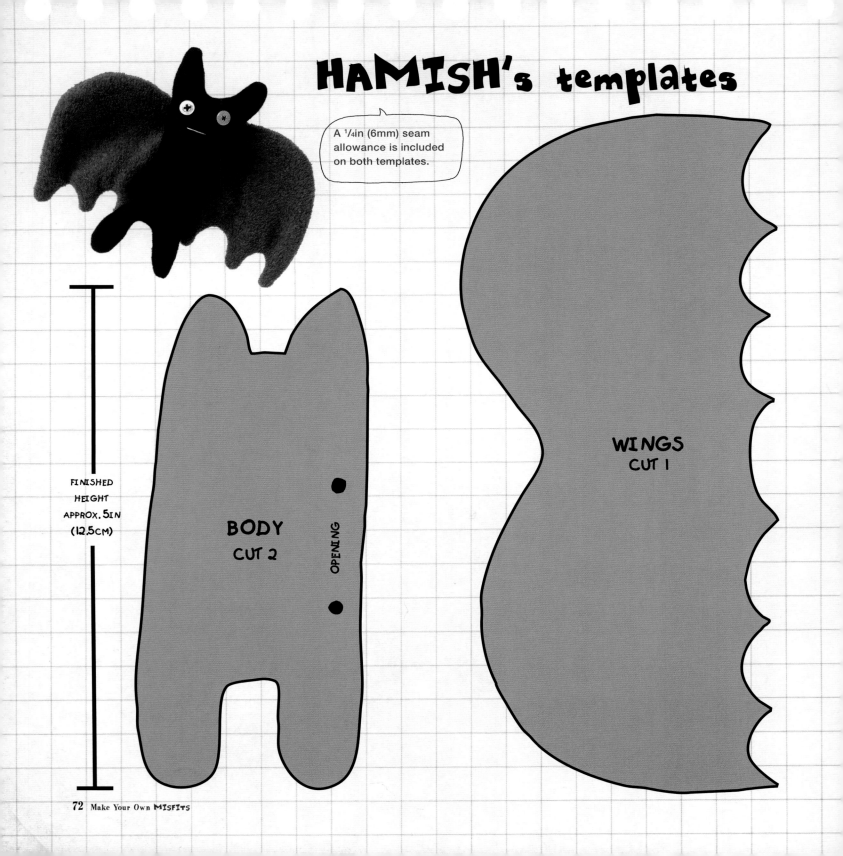

A ¼in (6mm) seam allowance is included on both templates.

FINISHED HEIGHT APPROX. 5IN (12.5CM)

BODY
CUT 2

OPENING

WINGS
CUT 1

MABEL the Duck

Mabel loves to swim in the pond but she would really like to fly, and one day, she knows, she will.

You will need...

BLUE TEE SHIRT	WHITE FLEECE SWEATER
ORANGE SOCK	SEWING MACHINE
MATCHING THREAD	WADDING
TWO BEADS	NOVELTY BUTTON

1. Using the templates on page 75, cut out two bodies from the tee shirt, two heads from the fleece, and two beaks from the sock. With a ¼in (6mm) seam allowance, machine stitch the matching pieces together, leaving a small opening in each piece.

2. Turn the body right side out and fill with wadding by pushing small amounts through the opening until it is nicely shaped. Use a stick or pencil to help push the wadding into the arms and legs. Do the same with the head and beak. Use an overhand stitch to sew up the openings in the head and body only.

3. Now it's time to stitch on the face. Using the diagram as a guide, stitch the beads on for eyes and sew the open end of the beak in place, using an overhand stitch.

4. Overhand stitch the head and the body together and finally, stitch on the novelty button for a brooch. Now she's ready for a paddle.

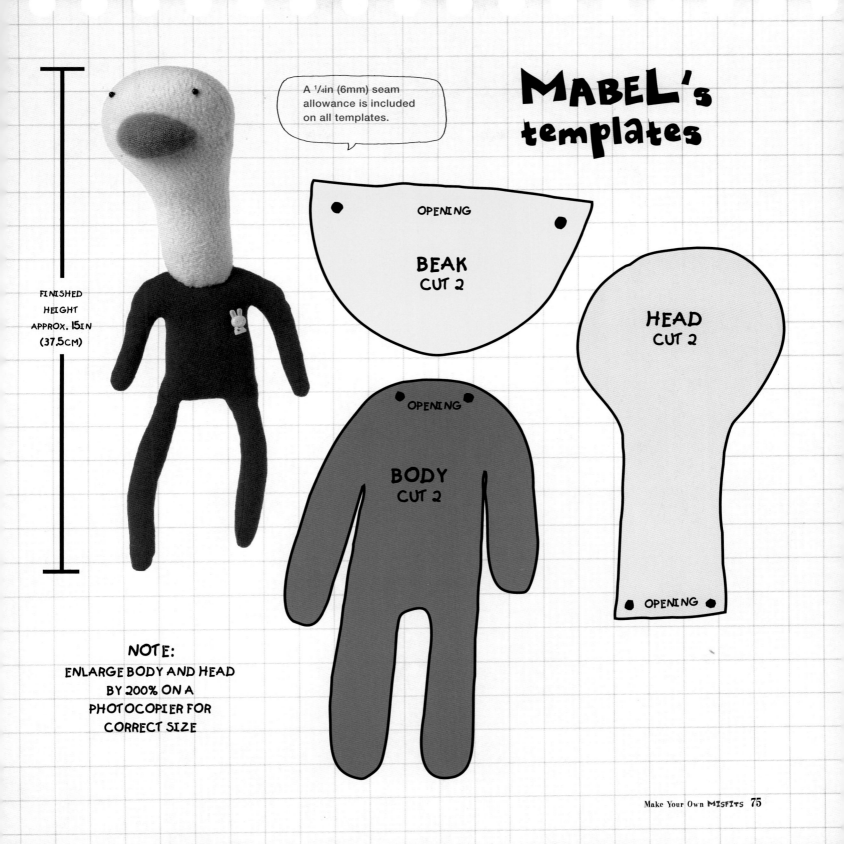

FINISHED HEIGHT APPROX. 15IN (37.5CM)

A ¼in (6mm) seam allowance is included on all templates.

MABEL's templates

OPENING

BEAK
CUT 2

HEAD
CUT 2

OPENING

BODY
CUT 2

OPENING

NOTE:
ENLARGE BODY AND HEAD
BY 200% ON A
PHOTOCOPIER FOR
CORRECT SIZE

AMAZON
the crocodile

Amazon sits very still and calm most of the time, but watch out as he can suddenly snap!

You will need...

GREEN TEE SHIRT

STRIPY TEE SHIRT

SEWING MACHINE

MATCHING THREAD

WADDING

TWO SHIRT BUTTONS

SCRAP OF WHITE FELT

NEEDLE

NOVELTY BUTTON

Using the templates on page 79, cut out two heads from the green tee shirt and two bodies from the stripy tee shirt. With a 1/4in (6mm) seam allowance, machine stitch the matching pieces together, leaving a small opening in each piece.

1

Turn the body right side out and fill with wadding by pushing small amounts through the opening until it is nicely shaped. Use a stick or pencil to help push the wadding into the arms and legs. Do the same with his head.

2

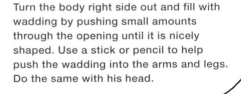

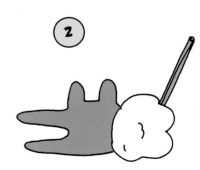

Use an overhand stitch to sew up the openings in the head and body.

3

Now it's time to stitch on his face. Using the diagram as a guide, stitch the two buttons on for eyes.

4

Using the template on page 79, cut out Amazon's teeth from felt and overhand stitch them to the top half of his mouth.

5

Overhand stitch the head and body together, and stitch the novelty button to his top to make him look smart. Now make sure you buy him a toothbrush, as he likes to keep his teeth shiny and bright.

6

AMAZON's templates

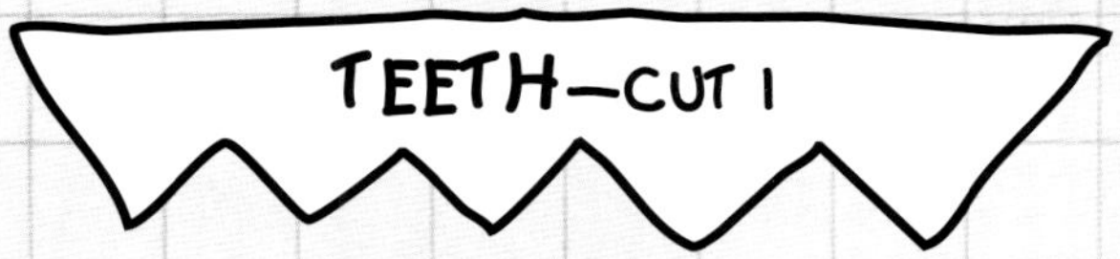

TEETH—CUT 1

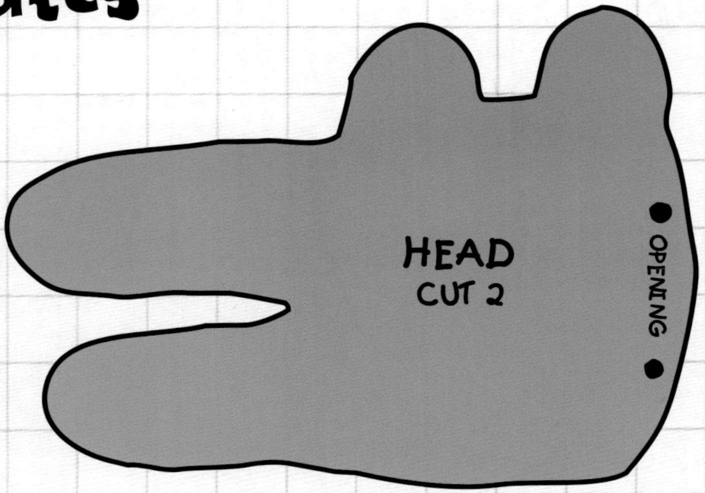

A ¼in (6mm) seam allowance is included on the body and head.

HEAD
CUT 2

● OPENING ●

FINISHED HEIGHT APPROX. 11IN (27.5CM)

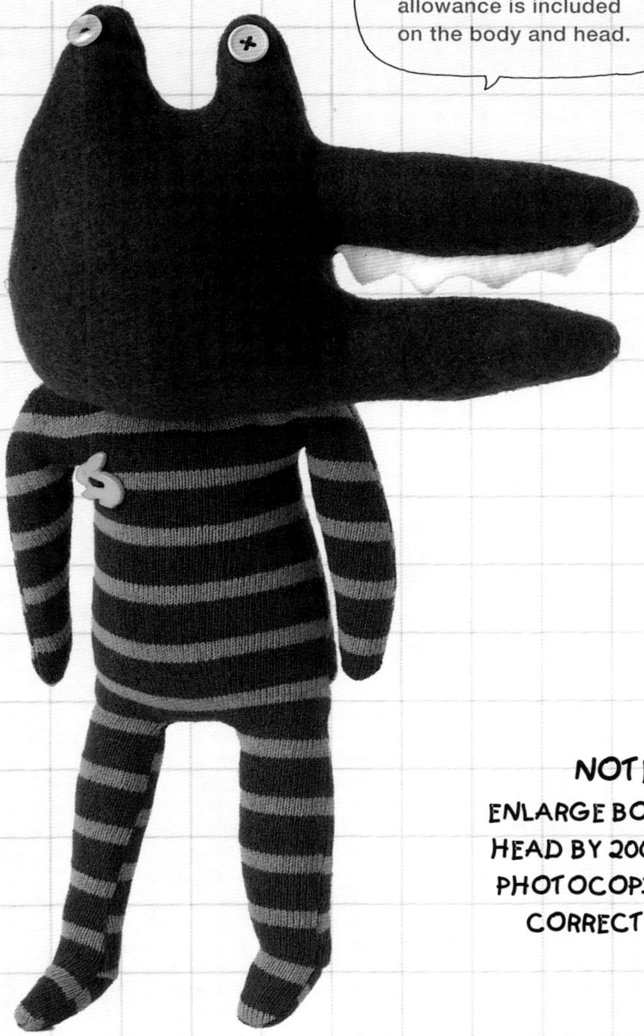

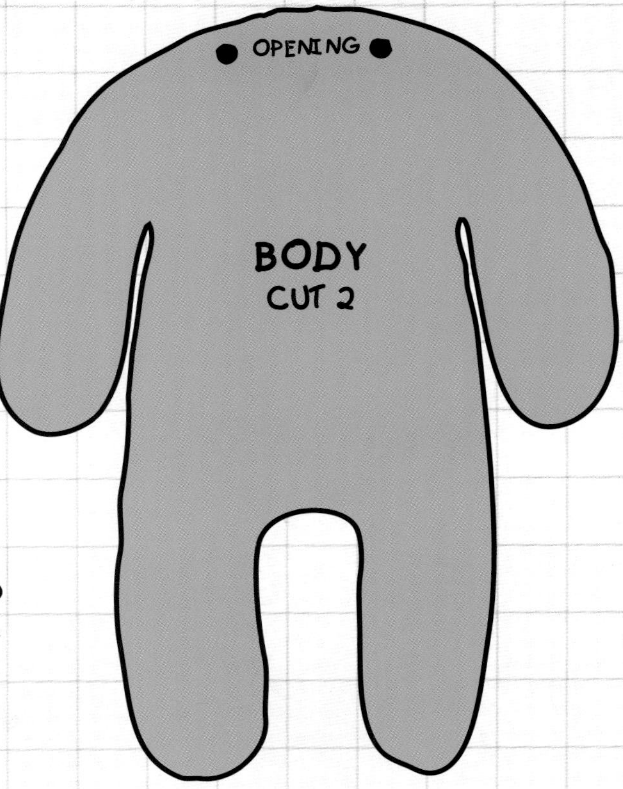

● OPENING ●

BODY
CUT 2

NOTE:
ENLARGE BODY AND
HEAD BY 200% ON A
PHOTOCOPIER FOR
CORRECT SIZE

WAN WAN the Panda

Wan Wan loves words and is never happier than when she's doing well on a crossword puzzle.

You will need...

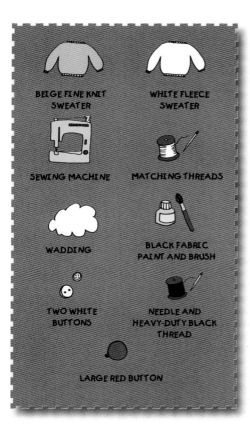

BEIGE FINE KNIT SWEATER

WHITE FLEECE SWEATER

SEWING MACHINE

MATCHING THREADS

WADDING

BLACK FABRIC PAINT AND BRUSH

TWO WHITE BUTTONS

NEEDLE AND HEAVY-DUTY BLACK THREAD

LARGE RED BUTTON

1

Using the templates on page 83, cut out two bodies from the sweater and two heads from the fleece. With a ¼in (6mm) seam allowance, machine stitch the matching pieces together, leaving a small opening in each piece.

2

Turn the body right side out and fill with wadding by pushing small amounts through the opening until it is nicely shaped. Use a stick or pencil to help push the wadding into the arms and legs. Do the same with her head.

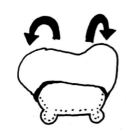

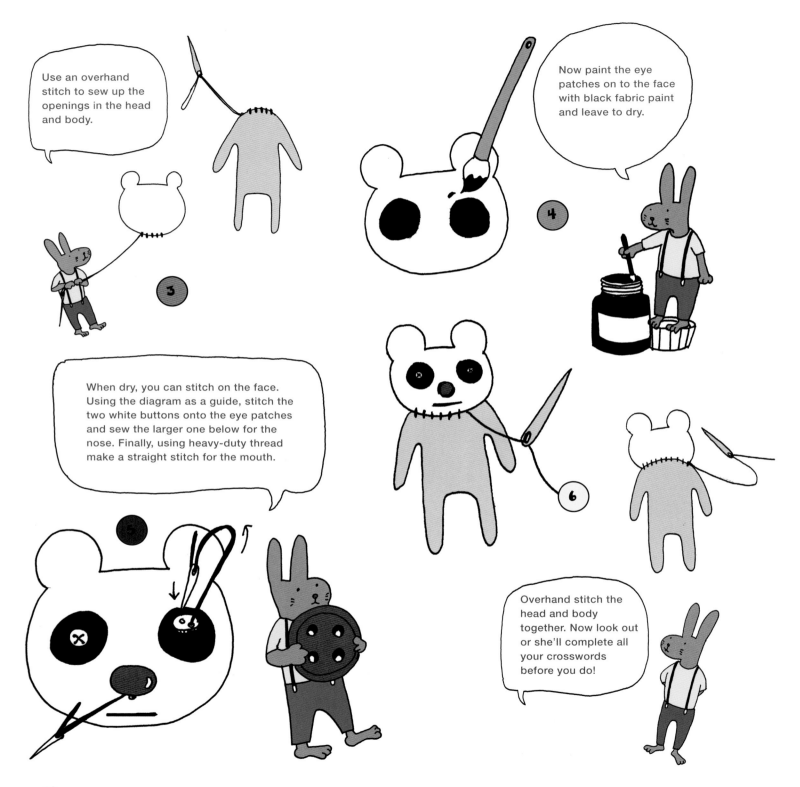

Use an overhand stitch to sew up the openings in the head and body.

Now paint the eye patches on to the face with black fabric paint and leave to dry.

When dry, you can stitch on the face. Using the diagram as a guide, stitch the two white buttons onto the eye patches and sew the larger one below for the nose. Finally, using heavy-duty thread make a straight stitch for the mouth.

Overhand stitch the head and body together. Now look out or she'll complete all your crosswords before you do!

WAN WAN's templates

A ¼in (6mm) seam allowance is included on both templates.

OPENING

BODY
CUT 2

FINISHED HEIGHT APPROX. 14IN (35CM)

NOTE:
ENLARGE BOTH
TEMPLATES BY 200% ON
A PHOTOCOPIER FOR
CORRECT SIZE

HEAD
CUT 2

OPENING

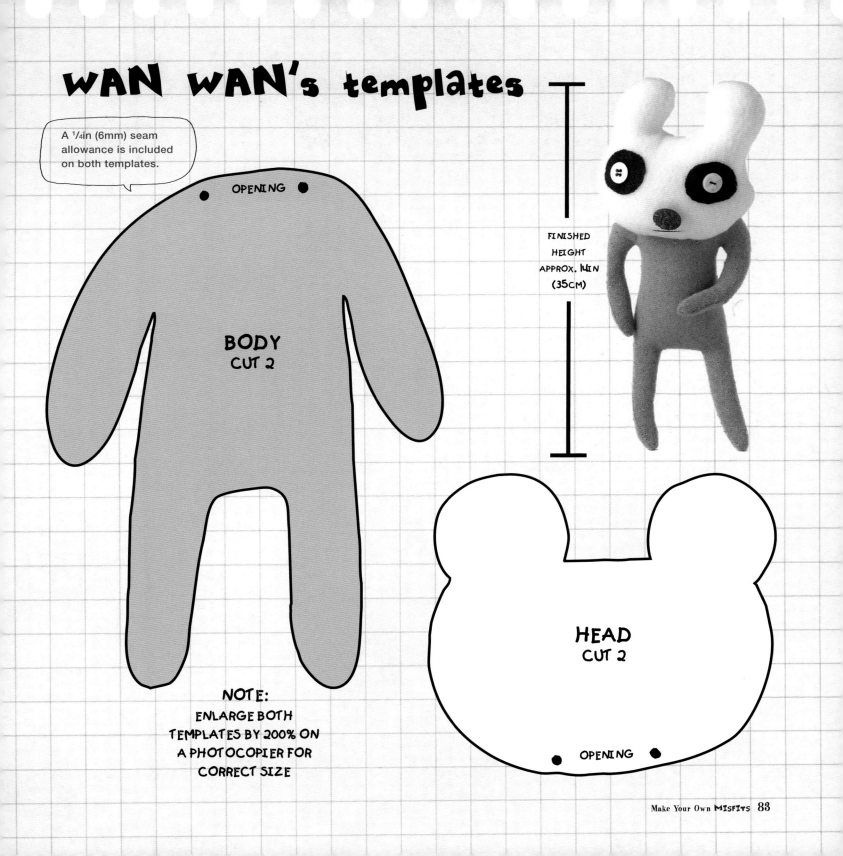

MAD HUNGRY wolf

Mad hungry wolf loves children, especially with rice 'n' peas!

You will need...

GRAY FLEECE SWEATER   BLACK TEE SHIRT

SEWING MACHINE   MATCHING THREAD

WADDING   TWO BUTTONS

SCRAP OF WHITE FELT   NEEDLE AND BLACK THREAD

Using the templates on page 87, cut out two heads from the fleece and two bodies from the tee shirt. Taking a ¼in (6mm) seam allowance, machine stitch the matching pieces together, leaving a small opening in each piece.

①

②

Turn the body right side out and fill with wadding by pushing small amounts through the opening until it is nicely shaped. Use a stick or pencil to help push the wadding into the arms and legs. Do the same with the head.

MAD HUNGRY's templates

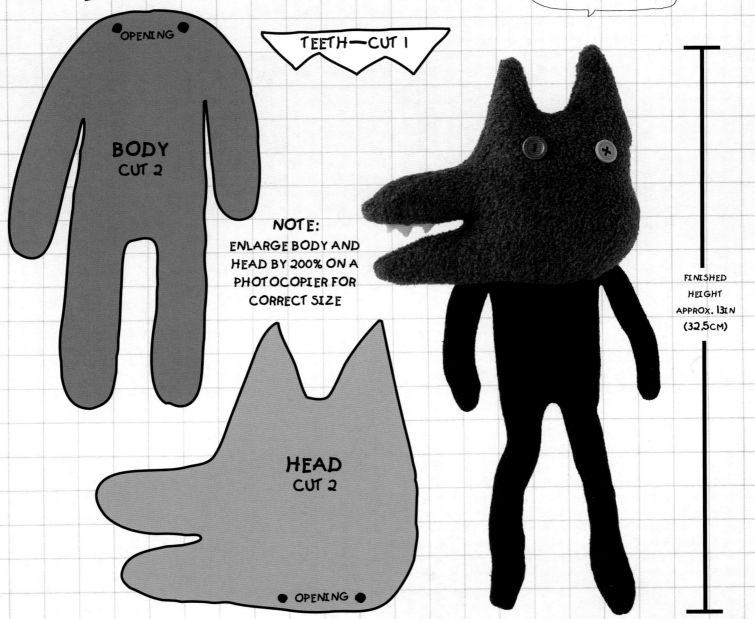

OPENING

TEETH—CUT 1

A ¼in (6mm) seam allowance is included on the body and head.

BODY
CUT 2

NOTE:
ENLARGE BODY AND
HEAD BY 200% ON A
PHOTOCOPIER FOR
CORRECT SIZE

HEAD
CUT 2

OPENING

FINISHED
HEIGHT
APPROX. 13IN
(32.5CM)

You will need...

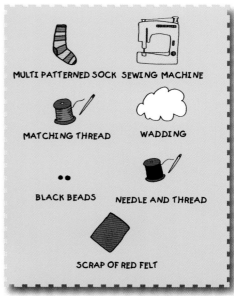

MULTI PATTERNED SOCK   SEWING MACHINE

MATCHING THREAD   WADDING

BLACK BEADS   NEEDLE AND THREAD

SCRAP OF RED FELT

SIDNEY the snake

Sidney likes nothing more than spending a hot summer day keeping cool and being quiet in a shaded and shadowy park.

Using the template opposite, cut out two of the body shape from the sock. With a ¼in (6mm) seam allowance, machine stitch the matching pieces together, leaving a small opening in each piece.

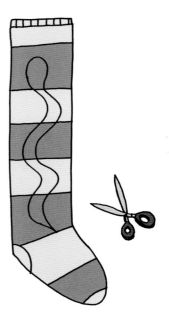

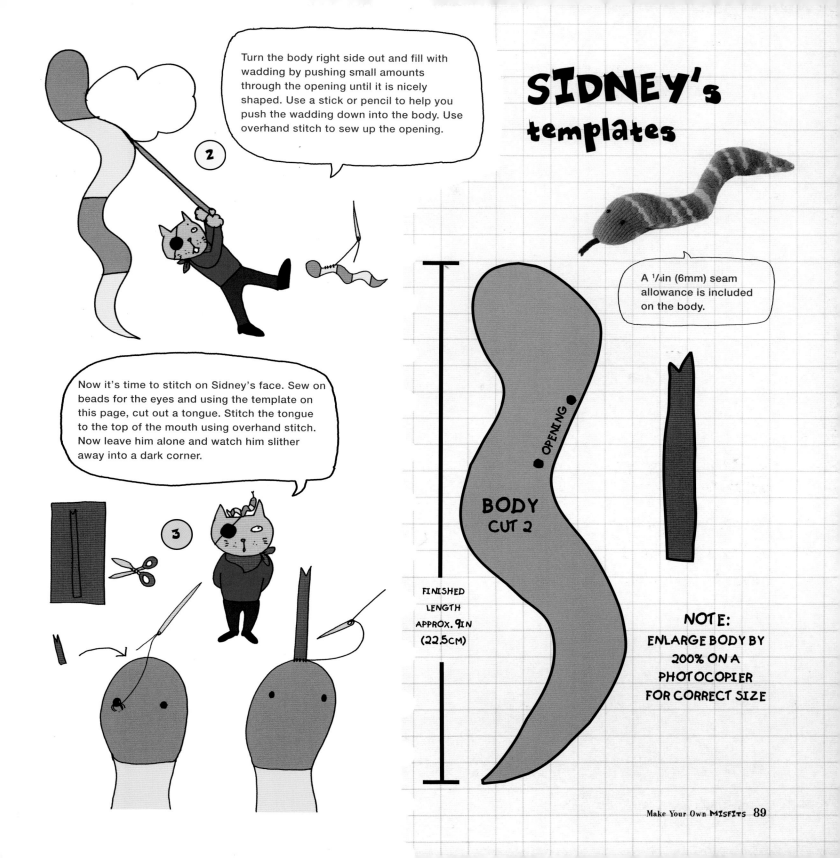

Turn the body right side out and fill with wadding by pushing small amounts through the opening until it is nicely shaped. Use a stick or pencil to help you push the wadding down into the body. Use overhand stitch to sew up the opening.

2

Now it's time to stitch on Sidney's face. Sew on beads for the eyes and using the template on this page, cut out a tongue. Stitch the tongue to the top of the mouth using overhand stitch. Now leave him alone and watch him slither away into a dark corner.

3

SIDNEY's templates

A ¼in (6mm) seam allowance is included on the body.

BODY CUT 2

OPENING

FINISHED LENGTH APPROX. 9IN (22.5CM)

NOTE: ENLARGE BODY BY 200% ON A PHOTOCOPIER FOR CORRECT SIZE

LORD ALBERT the lion

Lord Albert is a regal chap who takes himself very seriously. He reads many leather-bound books and his home smells of mahogany.

You will need...

RED TEE SHIRT

YELLOW TEE SHIRT

SEWING MACHINE

MATCHING THREADS

WADDING

TWO BLACK BEADS

LARGE FLAT BUTTON

NEEDLE AND BLACK HEAVY-DUTY THREAD

GREEN RIBBON

NOVELTY BUTTON

ORANGE FABRIC PAINT AND BRUSH

BLACK FABRIC PEN

1 Using the templates on page 93, cut out two bodies from the red tee shirt and two heads from the yellow tee shirt. With a ¼in (6mm) seam allowance, machine stitch the matching pieces together, leaving a small opening in each piece.

2 Turn the body right side out and fill with wadding by pushing small amounts through the opening until it is nicely shaped. Use a stick or pencil to help push the wadding into the arms and legs. Do the same with the head and then use an overhand stitch to sew up both openings.

Now it's time to stitch on the face. Using the diagram as a guide, stitch the beads on for eyes and the button below for the nose. Finally, with heavy-duty thread make three straight stitches for the mouth. Overhand stitch the head and body together.

3

Wrap the ribbon around Lord Albert's waist to form a belt and sew on the novelty button to keep it in place.

4

To complete Lord Albert, use the fabric paint to paint a mane around his face, and add spots with the fabric pen for his whiskers. Leave him to dry. Now just look at him, isn't he handsome?

5

LORD ALBERT's templates

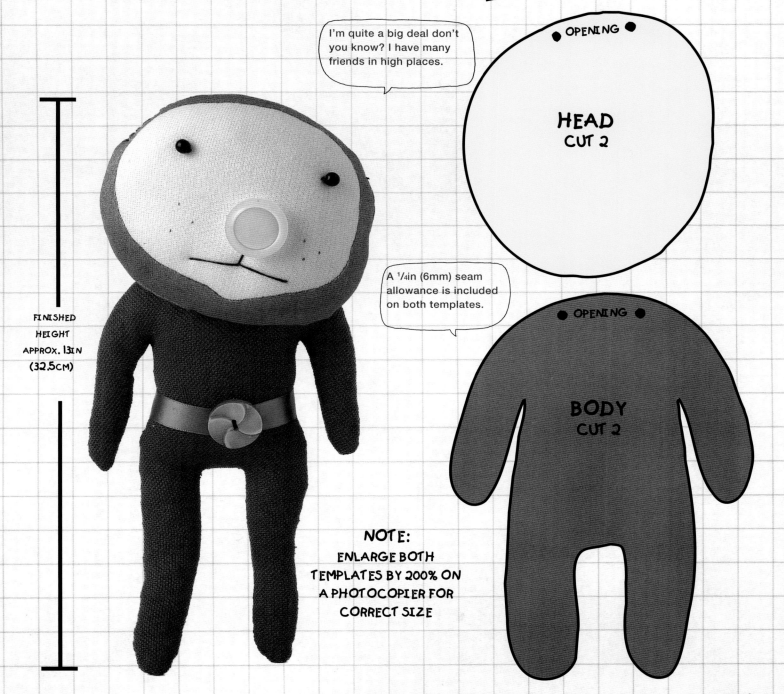

FINISHED HEIGHT APPROX. 13IN (32.5CM)

NOTE: ENLARGE BOTH TEMPLATES BY 200% ON A PHOTOCOPIER FOR CORRECT SIZE

MAKI the monkey

There's nothing this guy likes more than chilling out under a palm tree drinking from a coconut. Strangely he hates coconut milk, he's more of a margarita kind of monkey.

You will need...

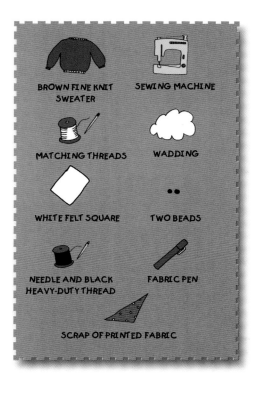

BROWN FINE KNIT SWEATER

SEWING MACHINE

MATCHING THREADS

WADDING

WHITE FELT SQUARE

TWO BEADS

NEEDLE AND BLACK HEAVY-DUTY THREAD

FABRIC PEN

SCRAP OF PRINTED FABRIC

Using the templates on page 97, cut out two heads and two bodies from the sweater. With a ¼in (6mm) seam allowance, machine stitch the matching pieces together, leaving a small opening in each piece.

2

Turn the body right side out and fill with wadding by pushing small amounts through the opening until it is nicely shaped. Use a stick or pencil to help push the wadding into the arms and legs. Do the same with the head.

Use an overhand stitch to sew up the openings in the body and head.

3

Now it's time to stitch Maki's face. Using the template opposite, cut out one face from felt. Then, using the diagram as a guide, stitch on two beads for eyes and make a large stitch below for the mouth with the heavy-duty thread. Finally, draw on two nostrils using the fabric pen.

4

Sew the outer edges of the completed face to the front of the head, using overhand stitch.

5

Attach the head to the body using overhand stitch and finish off with a strip of the printed fabric tied around his neck. Now leave him to chill.

6

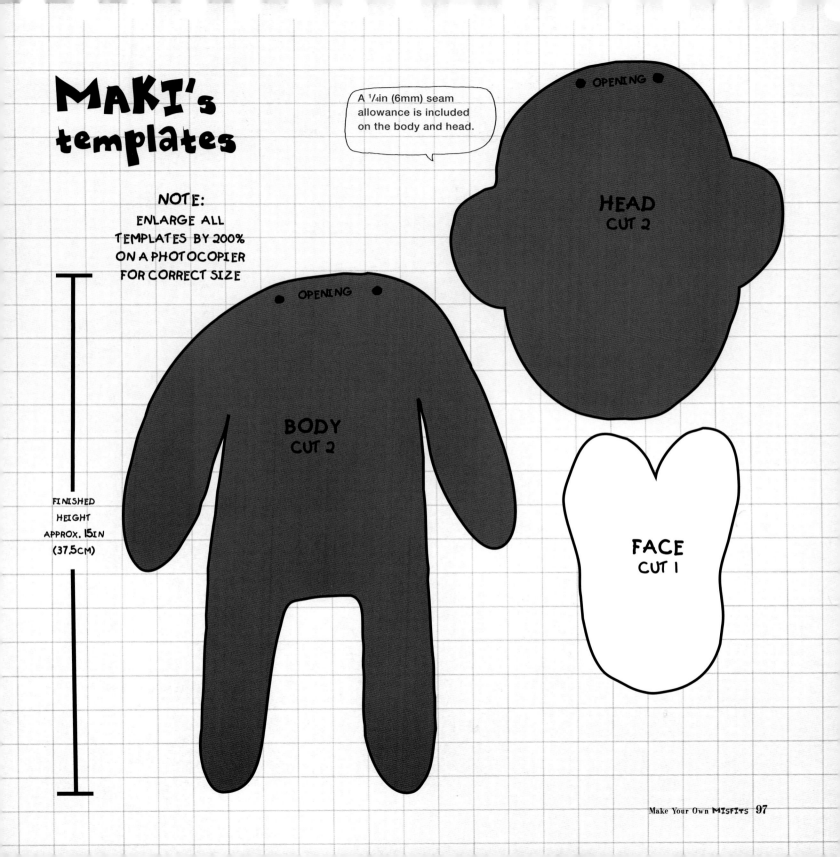

QUICKSILVER
the retired racehorse

Quicksilver used to be a racehorse but now he's too old. Although he retired many years ago, he is full of stories from past travels, so come, sit close, and listen to some of his wonderful adventures.

You will need...

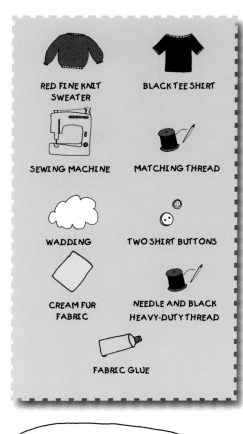

RED FINE KNIT SWEATER

BLACK TEE SHIRT

SEWING MACHINE

MATCHING THREAD

WADDING

TWO SHIRT BUTTONS

CREAM FUR FABRIC

NEEDLE AND BLACK HEAVY-DUTY THREAD

FABRIC GLUE

Using the templates on page 101, cut out two bodies from the tee shirt and two heads from the sweater. With a ¼in (6mm) seam allowance, machine stitch the matching pieces together, leaving a small opening in each piece.

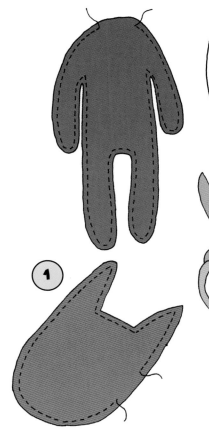

1

Turn the body right side out and fill with wadding by pushing small amounts through the opening until it is nicely shaped. Use a stick or pencil to help push the wadding into the arms and legs. Do the same with the head.

2

Use overhand stitch to sew up the openings in the body and the head.

3

4

Now it's time to stitch on the face. Using the diagram as a guide, stitch on buttons for eyes. Then, using the heavy-duty thread make a large stitch around the base of the head to define the nose section, stitch two nostrils below the line, and then add a mouth.

Using the templates opposite for the mane, cut a long rectangle of fur fabric to go between the ears and right down the back of the head; glue in place. Cut another small piece for the tail.

5

When the mane is dry, overhand stitch the head and body together then either glue or stitch the tail in place. Now Quicksilver's finished he's yours to keep. So feed him with cups of tea and in return he'll tell you tales from the olden days to make your head spin!

6

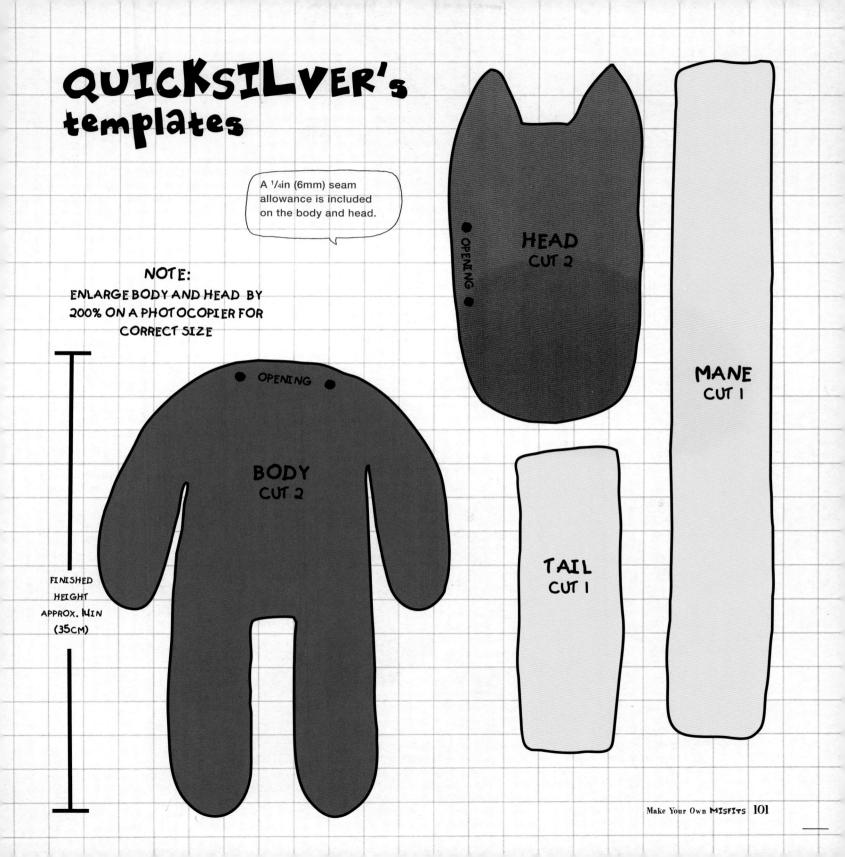

GOLDIE the fish

Goldie likes things to be really simple, just the way they are. That's because he's such an easy fellow for you to make—you can finish him in minutes!

Using the template on page 103, cut out two bodies. Taking a ¼in (6mm) seam allowance, machine stitch the pieces together, leaving a small opening for turning through.

You will need...

ORANGE SOCK

SEWING MACHINE

MATCHING THREAD

WADDING

TWO SHIRT BUTTONS

NEEDLE AND BLACK HEAVY-DUTY THREAD

2

Turn the body right side out and fill with wadding by pushing small amounts through the opening until it is nicely shaped. Use overhand stitch to sew up the opening.

A ¼in (6mm) seam allowance is included.

GOLDIE's
templates

Now it's time to stitch on the face. Using the photograph as a guide, stitch on the buttons for eyes and make a long stitch for his mouth using the heavy-duty thread. That's it, he's that simple and that's the way he likes it!

3

BODY
CUT 2

OPENING

FINISHED HEIGHT APPROX. 3IN (7.5CM)

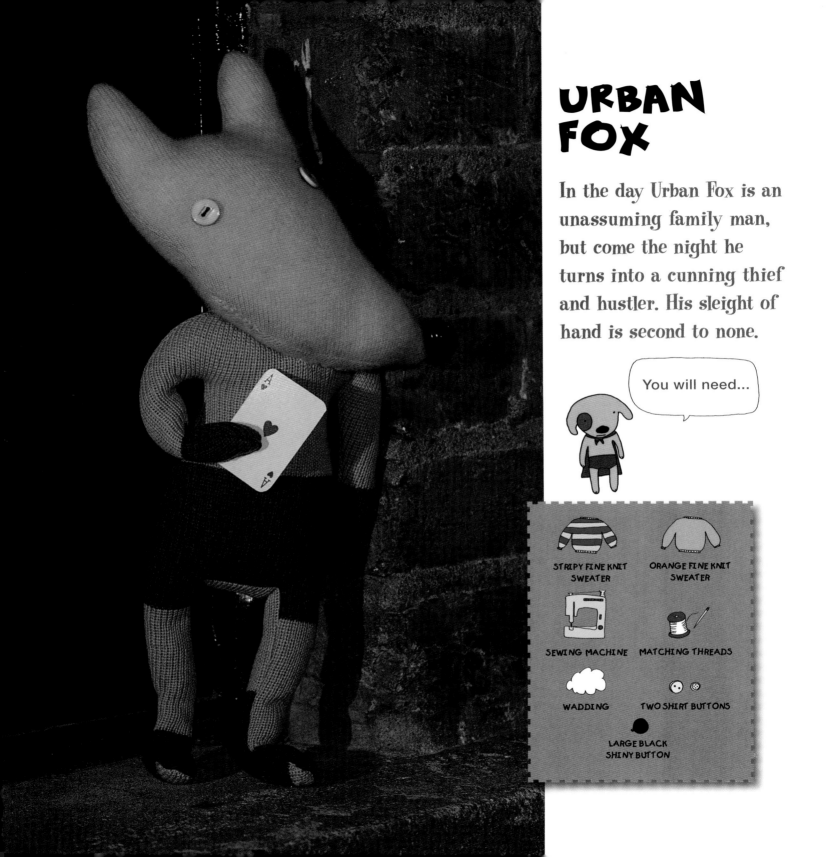

URBAN FOX

In the day Urban Fox is an unassuming family man, but come the night he turns into a cunning thief and hustler. His sleight of hand is second to none.

You will need...

STRIPY FINE KNIT
SWEATER

ORANGE FINE KNIT
SWEATER

SEWING MACHINE

MATCHING THREADS

WADDING

TWO SHIRT BUTTONS

LARGE BLACK
SHINY BUTTON

Using the templates on page 106, cut out two bodies from the stripy sweater and two heads from the orange sweater. With a ¼in (6mm) seam allowance, machine stitch the matching pieces together, leaving a small opening in each piece.

Turn the body right side out and fill with wadding by pushing small amounts through the opening until it is nicely shaped. Use a stick or pencil to help push the wadding into the arms and legs. Do the same with the head.

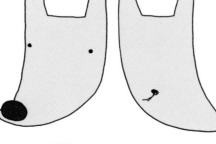

Use an overhand stitch to sew up the openings in the body and head.

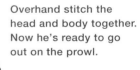

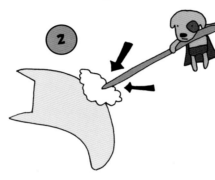

Now it's time to stitch on the face. Using the photograph as a guide, stitch on the smaller buttons for the eyes and the larger button for the nose.

Overhand stitch the head and body together. Now he's ready to go out on the prowl.

URBAN FOX's templates

NOTE:
ENLARGE BOTH TEMPLATES BY 200% ON A PHOTOCOPIER FOR CORRECT SIZE

HEAD
CUT 2

OPENING

OPENING

FINISHED HEIGHT APPROX. 17IN (42.5CM)

BODY
CUT 2

OPENING

A ¼in (6mm) seam allowance is included on both templates.

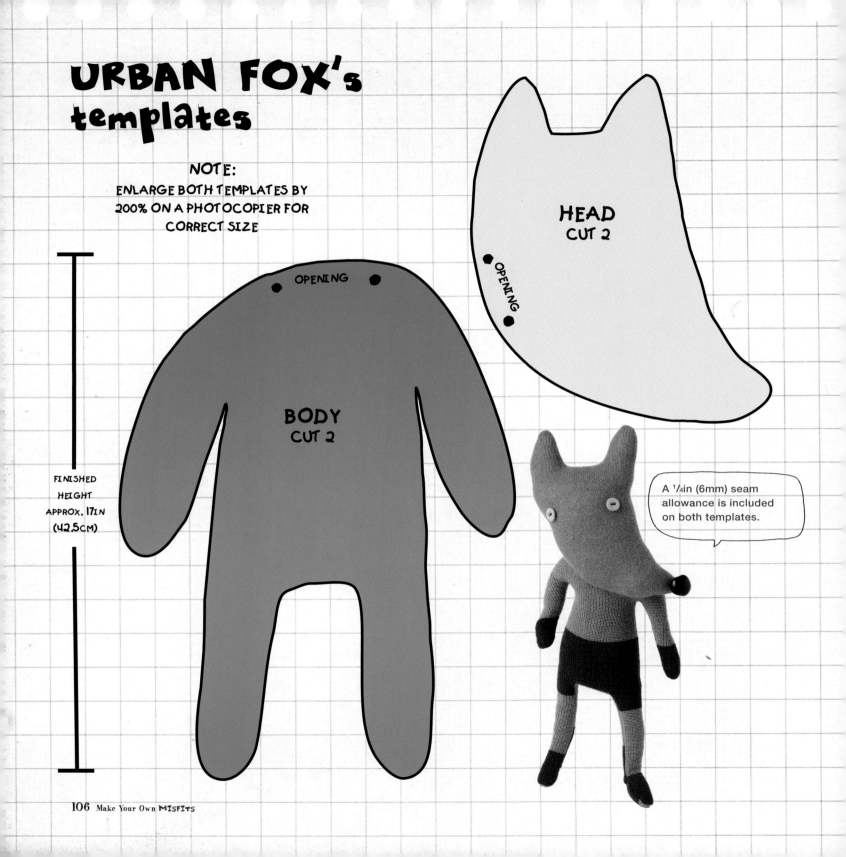

SAKURA the chicken

Sakura's a real mother hen, always taking care of little chicks and cooking up a storm in the kitchen.

You will need...

BLUE TEE SHIRT   WHITE FELT SQUARES

ORANGE SOCK   RED SOCK

SEWING MACHINE   MATCHING THREAD

WADDING   TWO BLACK BEADS

NEEDLE AND THREAD

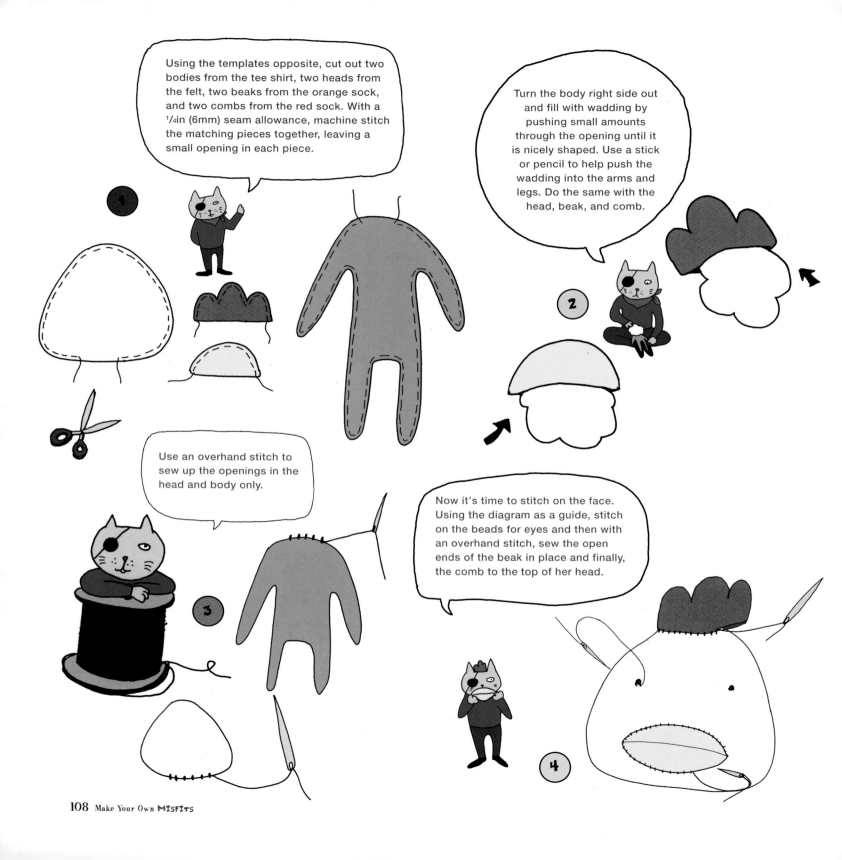

Using the templates opposite, cut out two bodies from the tee shirt, two heads from the felt, two beaks from the orange sock, and two combs from the red sock. With a ¼in (6mm) seam allowance, machine stitch the matching pieces together, leaving a small opening in each piece.

1

Turn the body right side out and fill with wadding by pushing small amounts through the opening until it is nicely shaped. Use a stick or pencil to help push the wadding into the arms and legs. Do the same with the head, beak, and comb.

2

Use an overhand stitch to sew up the openings in the head and body only.

3

Now it's time to stitch on the face. Using the diagram as a guide, stitch on the beads for eyes and then with an overhand stitch, sew the open ends of the beak in place and finally, the comb to the top of her head.

4

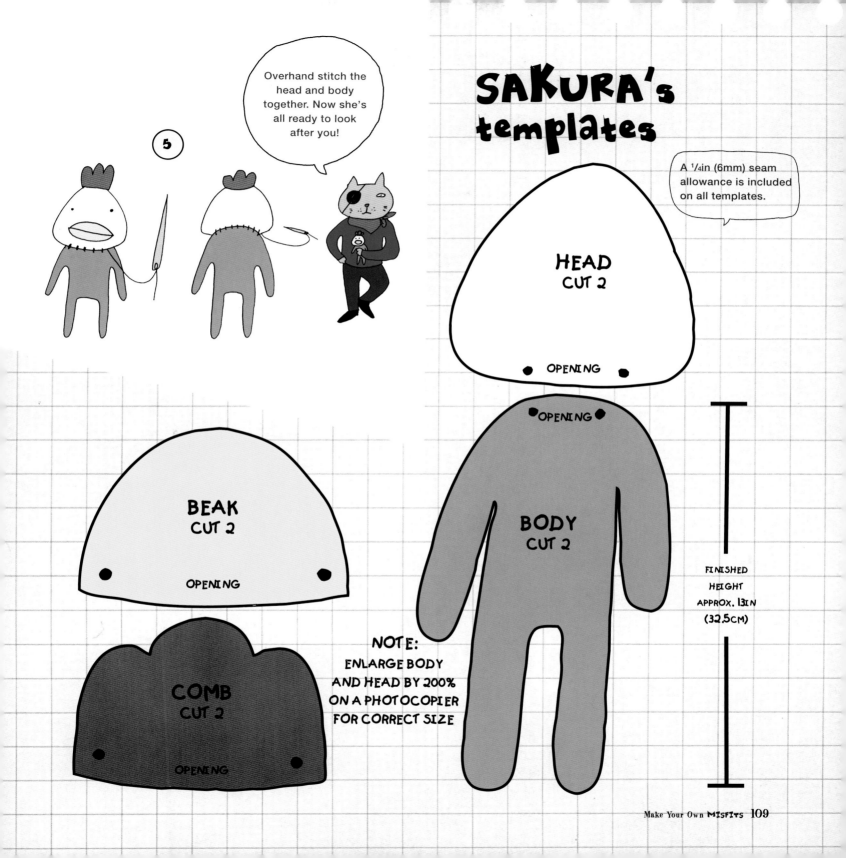

SAKURA's templates

SATOKO
the raccoon

Satoko spends all summer knitting her wardrobe ready for the winter. Her kids aren't so keen though on the sweaters she makes for them at Christmas.

You will need...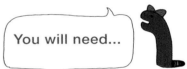

BEIGE FINE KNIT SWEATER

STRIPY SWEATER

SEWING MACHINE

MATCHING THREADS

WADDING

SCRAP OF BLACK FELT

FABRIC GLUE

TWO BEIGE BUTTONS

LEATHER BUTTON

NEEDLE AND BLACK HEAVY-DUTY THREAD

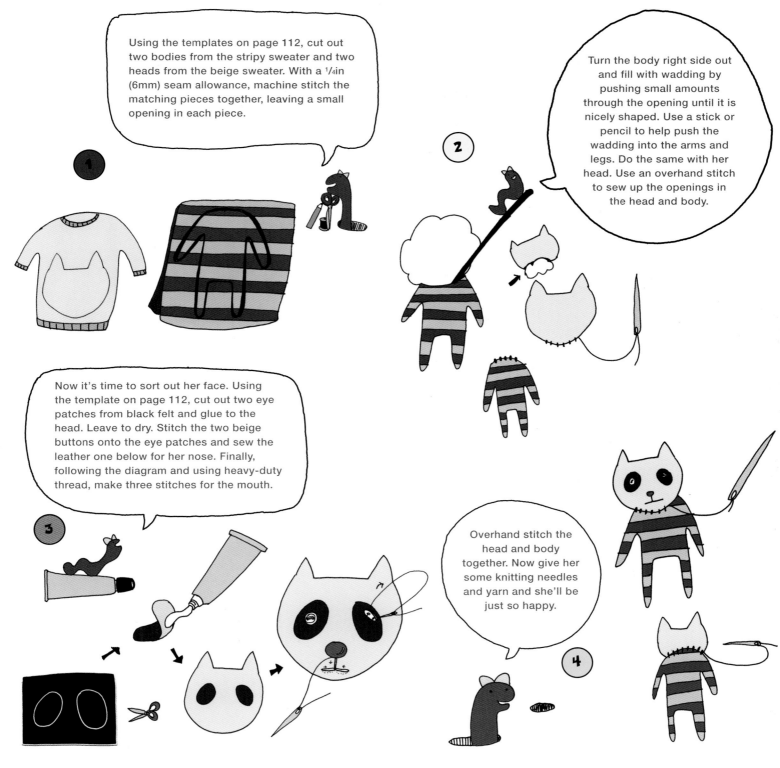

1. Using the templates on page 112, cut out two bodies from the stripy sweater and two heads from the beige sweater. With a ¼in (6mm) seam allowance, machine stitch the matching pieces together, leaving a small opening in each piece.

2. Turn the body right side out and fill with wadding by pushing small amounts through the opening until it is nicely shaped. Use a stick or pencil to help push the wadding into the arms and legs. Do the same with her head. Use an overhand stitch to sew up the openings in the head and body.

3. Now it's time to sort out her face. Using the template on page 112, cut out two eye patches from black felt and glue to the head. Leave to dry. Stitch the two beige buttons onto the eye patches and sew the leather one below for her nose. Finally, following the diagram and using heavy-duty thread, make three stitches for the mouth.

4. Overhand stitch the head and body together. Now give her some knitting needles and yarn and she'll be just so happy.

SATOKO's templates

NOTE:
ENLARGE BODY AND HEAD BY
200% ON A PHOTOCOPIER FOR
CORRECT SIZE

LEFT
EYE
PATCH
CUT 1

A ¼in (6mm) seam
allowance is included on
the body, head.

RIGHT
EYE
PATCH
CUT 1

OPENING

BODY
CUT 2

FINISHED
HEIGHT
APPROX. 16IN
(40CM)

HEAD
CUT 2

OPENING

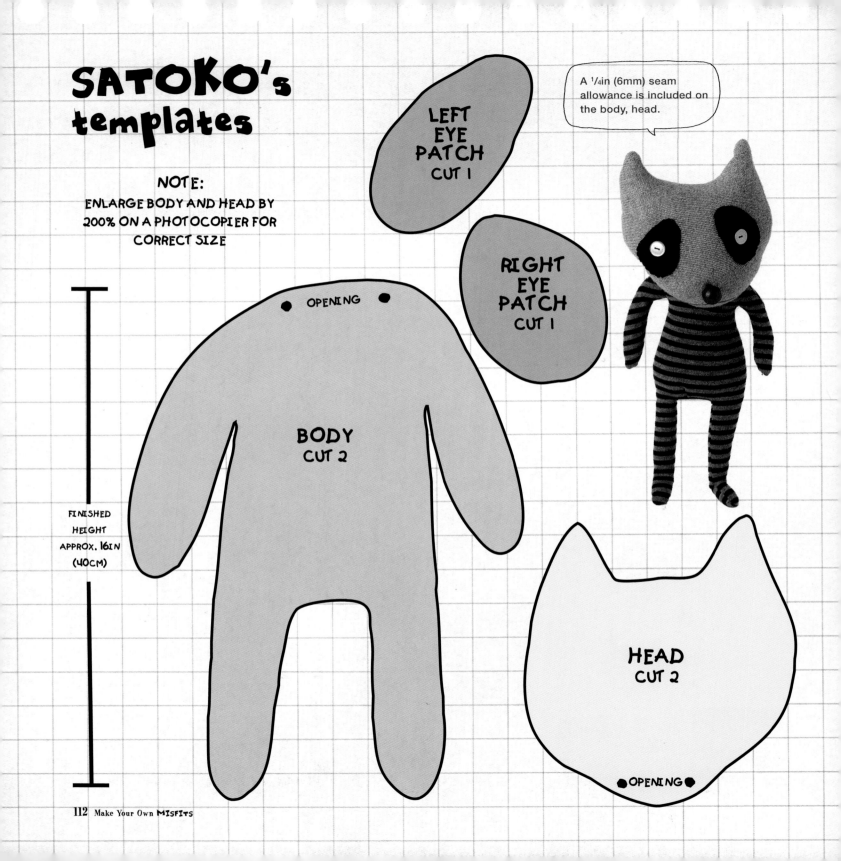

ROXY the bear

Roxy is a vinyl junkie with an enormous record collection. She loves to go to concerts in massive stadiums and rock out to heavy metal music.

You will need...

PATTERNED TEE SHIRT	FUR FABRIC
SEWING MACHINE	RED SOCK
WADDING	MATCHING THREADS
RIBBON FLOWER MOTIF	NEEDLE AND BLACK HEAVY-DUTY THREAD
TWO BLACK BUTTONS	NARROW RIBBON

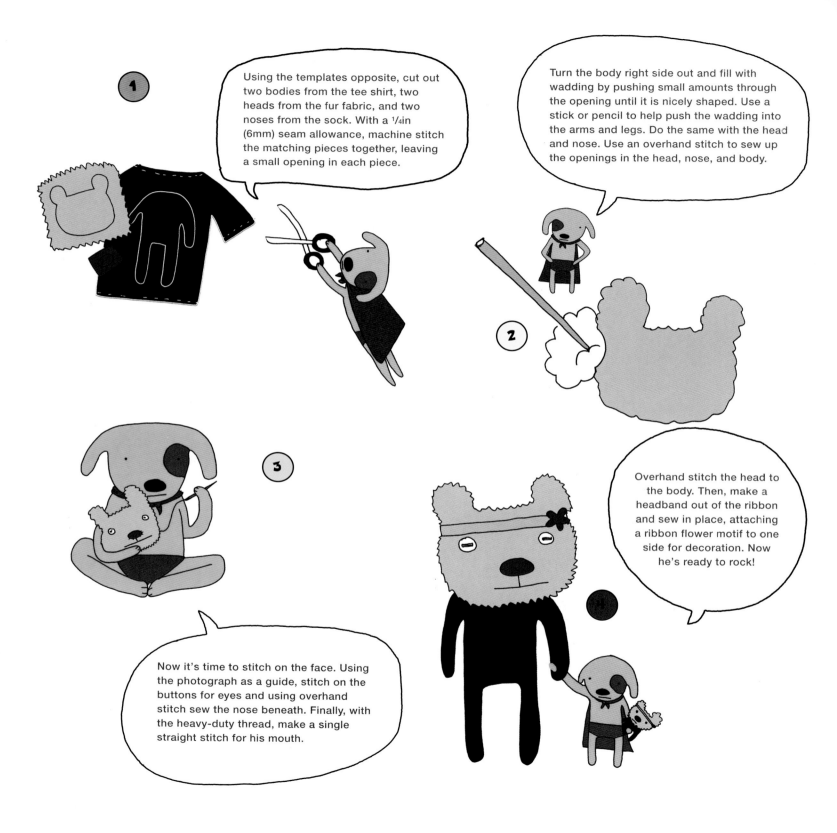

ROXY's templates

NOTE:
ENLARGE BODY AND HEAD BY 200% ON A PHOTOCOPIER FOR CORRECT SIZE

NOSE
CUT 2

OPENING

HEAD
CUT 2

OPENING

OPENING

OPENING

BODY
CUT 2

FINISHED HEIGHT APPROX. 18IN (45CM)

A ¼in (6mm) seam allowance is included on all templates.

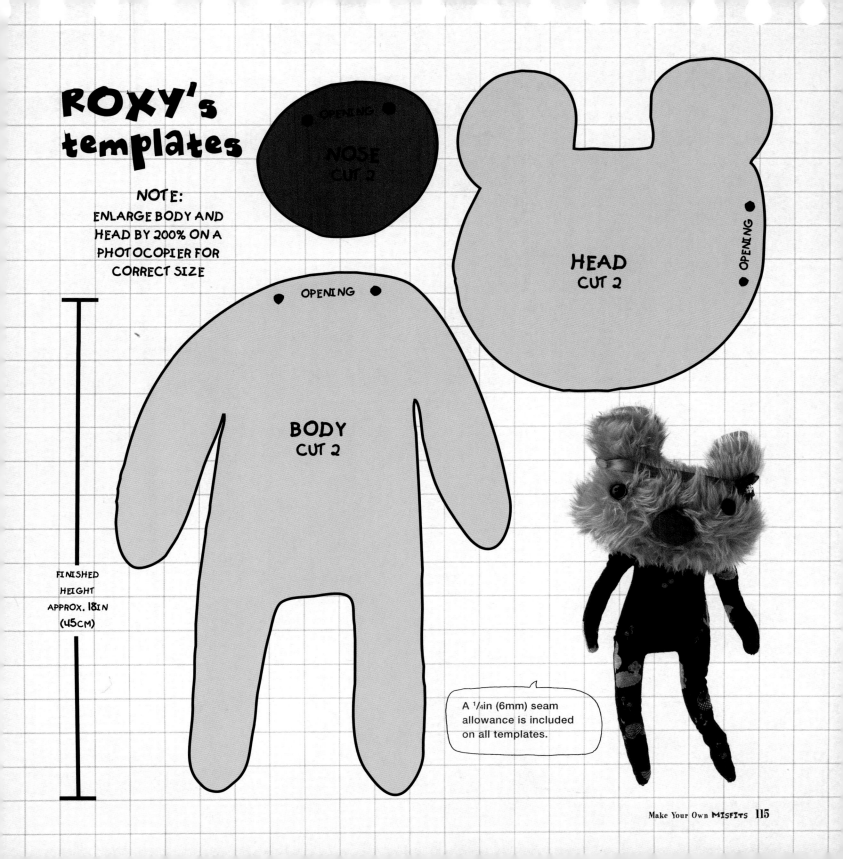

BUSTER the beaver

Buster is a really cheeky chap, who's always planning his next practical joke. He's a talented cartoonist and his caricatures will certainly make you laugh.

You will need...

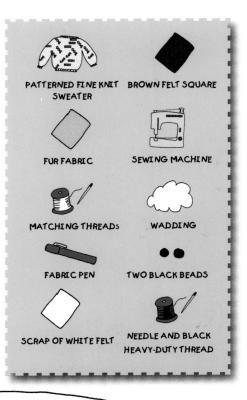

- PATTERNED FINE KNIT SWEATER
- BROWN FELT SQUARE
- FUR FABRIC
- SEWING MACHINE
- MATCHING THREADS
- WADDING
- FABRIC PEN
- TWO BLACK BEADS
- SCRAP OF WHITE FELT
- NEEDLE AND BLACK HEAVY-DUTY THREAD

1 Using the templates on page 119, cut out two bodies from the sweater, two heads from the fur fabric, and two noses from the felt. With a ¼in (6mm) seam allowance, machine stitch the matching pieces together, leaving a small opening in each piece.

2 Turn the body right side out and fill with wadding by pushing small amounts through the opening until it is nicely shaped. Use a stick or pencil to help push the wadding into the arms and legs. Do the same with the head and nose. Use an overhand stitch to sew up the openings in the head, nose, and body.

Now it's time to stitch on the face. Using the diagram as a guide, stitch on the beads for eyes and sew the nose in place, using overhand stitch. Then, make three straight stitches for the mouth, using the heavy-duty thread.

Using the template opposite, cut out Buster's teeth from felt. Draw a line down the center with the fabric pen and then stitch the teeth in place, just below his mouth.

3

4

Use overhand stitch to sew the head and body together. Now watch out, as he'll have you in fits of giggles all day and you won't get anything done!

5

BUSTER's templates

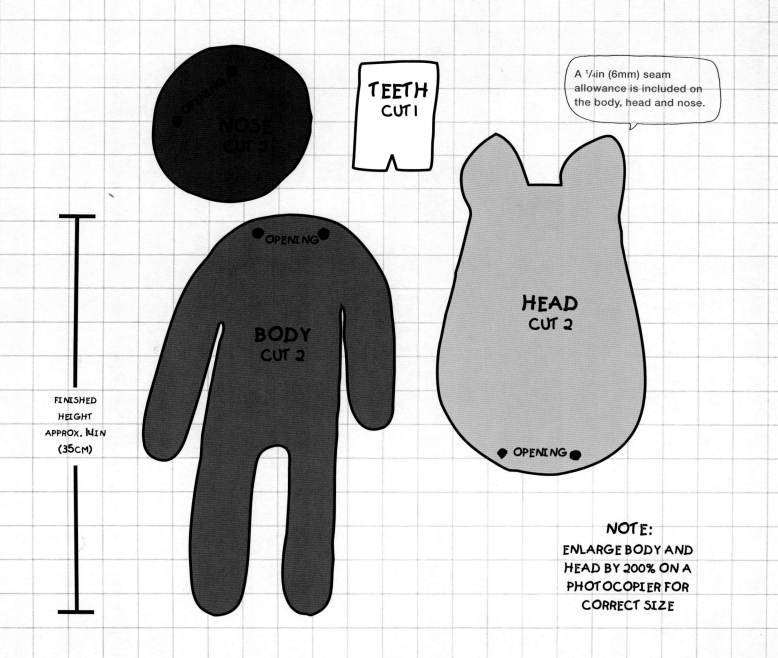

NOSE
CUT 2

OPENING

TEETH
CUT 1

A ¼in (6mm) seam allowance is included on the body, head and nose.

OPENING

BODY
CUT 2

HEAD
CUT 2

OPENING

FINISHED HEIGHT APPROX. 14IN (35CM)

NOTE:
ENLARGE BODY AND HEAD BY 200% ON A PHOTOCOPIER FOR CORRECT SIZE

TONY the sausage dog

Tony would love to be a stunt dog. He doesn't walk on the ground like ordinary folk, he jumps, climbs, and free falls along walls and fences. One day he'll just pack his bags and go to Hollywood to be a star.

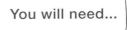

You will need...

BROWN FINE KIT SWEATER

BLACK SOCK

SEWING MACHINE

MATCHING THREAD

WADDING

TWO SHIRT BUTTONS

NEEDLE AND WHITE HEAVY-DUTY THREAD

SCRAP OF SPOTTY FABRIC

1

Turn the body right side out and fill with wadding by pushing small amounts through the opening until it is nicely shaped. Use a stick or pencil to help push the wadding into the arms and legs. Do the same with Tony's head and nose.

Using the templates on page 123, cut out two bodies and two heads from the sweater and two noses from the sock. With a ¼in (6mm) seam allowance, machine stitch the matching pieces together, leaving a small opening in each piece.

2

TONY's templates

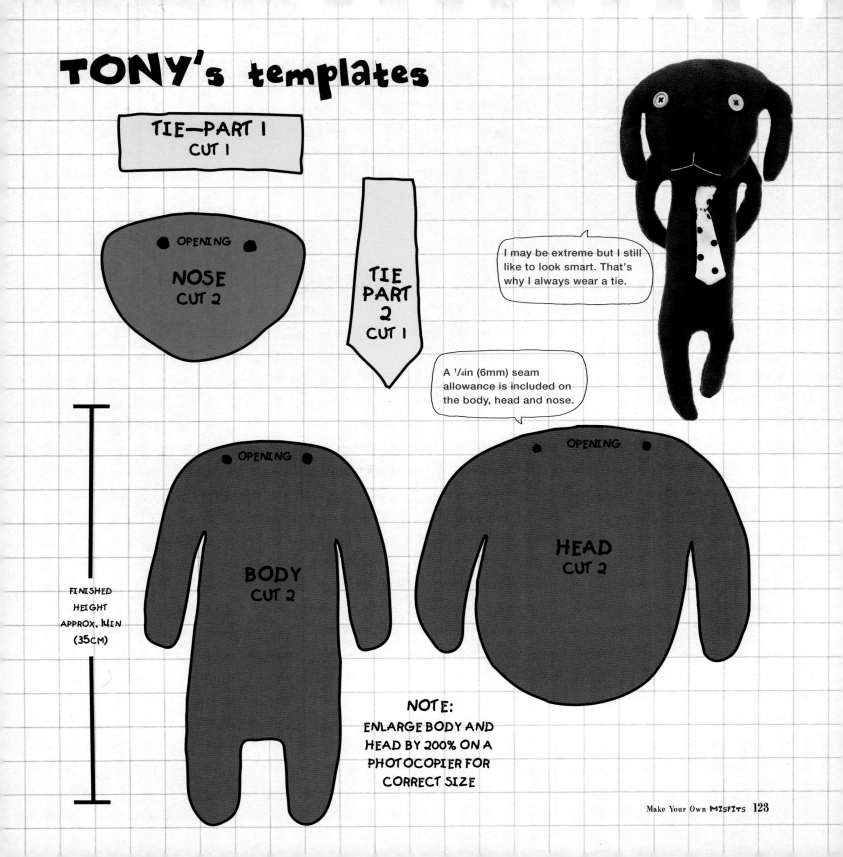

TIE—PART 1
CUT 1

NOSE
CUT 2

OPENING

TIE PART 2
CUT 1

I may be extreme but I still like to look smart. That's why I always wear a tie.

A ¼in (6mm) seam allowance is included on the body, head and nose.

BODY
CUT 2

OPENING

HEAD
CUT 2

OPENING

FINISHED HEIGHT APPROX. 14IN (35CM)

NOTE:
ENLARGE BODY AND HEAD BY 200% ON A PHOTOCOPIER FOR CORRECT SIZE

Techniques

Making your own misfit is a pretty simple process and you'll only need to get to grips with a few techniques to start making dolls that look as good as the ones in the photographs.

Who would have thought making something as handsome as me would be so easy!

Overhand stitch

We use this one for nearly everything, including sewing up holes and stitching on heads and noses.

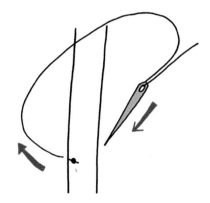

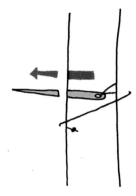

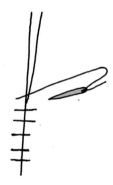

1 Thread the needle and tie a knot in the end. Bring the needle to the front on one side then take it across at a slight diagonal to the opposite edge.

2 Take the needle down and straight back across to the opposite edge, pulling the edges together. Keep stitching from left to right, drawing the edges together.

3 Repeat this all the way along, making sure your stitches are the same length by tying a knot at the end on the wrong side of the fabric.

Sewing on a button

We love our buttons and buttons love misfits!
Here's how to stitch them on.

Looks easy enough!

1 Thread the needle and tie a knot in the end. Place the button on top of the material where you intend to sew it in place. Push the needle up through the material and one of the button holes.

2 Pull all the way through until the knot is anchored against the material. Push the needle down through the next hole on the button and through the material.

3 Keep going up and down through the hole on the button and through the material. Secure it with a knot.

Sewing on a bead

Beads make wise eyes, so here's how to stitch them on.

1 Anchor the thread to the back of the fabric and pull the needle through to the front. Slip a bead onto the threaded needle and pull down so it's sitting where you want it to be.

2 Bring the needle back through the fabric and out again and through the eye of the bead and back through the fabric.

3 Repeat a few times until it's fixed on nice and securely and knot off.

Index

Acknowledgments

Thank you to Fumie's Mum, Dad, and Grandma, and to Rosie's Mum and Dad for helping and supporting us. A big thank you also to Tony, our right-hand man.